Dear Family Member,

Sight words are those frequently used, non-decodable words that are essential to reading fluency. Ask any teacher or educational expert what's the only way for children to master these sight words and they'll all agree—practice!

We've created the *Scholastic 100 Words* workbook series to give your child that practice. Working with literacy specialists and classroom teachers, we identified the 100 sight words your child needs to know by second grade. Then we developed inviting educational activities to give your child opportunities to read, write, and use these words.

The sight words in Scholastic's *100 Words Kids Need to Read by 2nd Grade* are divided into seven word groups. The words in each group are introduced in context and reinforced throughout the activities. As your child moves through this workbook, he or she will move from visual recognition of sight words to genuine mastery. Your child will also gain important preparatory experience that will later help with standardized tests.

To reinforce the message that skill-building helps make reading fluent—*and fun*—we've included a wonderful "mini-book" at the end of each word group section. This mini-book weaves all the words from the word group into a lively story your child will love reading aloud. And to encourage your child's love of reading, we've also included a poster listing 100 Great Books for 2nd Graders.

The journey through these workbook pages will help young readers make the successful transition from learning to read to reading to learn. Enjoy the trip!

David Goddy
Publisher, Scholastic Magazines

Tips For Family Members

Join in with your child on the activity pages:
- ✓ Read the directions aloud.
- ✓ Help your child get started by making sure he or she knows what to do.
- ✓ Point out examples, such as circles or underlines, in the directions. Show your child how to use the illustrations or photos to provide clues for words.

Share the mini-books with your child:
- ✓ To assemble a mini-book, detach the four pages where perforated. Put the first two pages back to back, pictures facing out. Fold on the dotted line. Do the same with the second two pages. Insert the second set into the first set. The mini-book cover will be on the outside; story pages will follow in number order.
- ✓ Ask your child to read the story aloud to you. Using the word list on page 3, ask your child to find all the words from the word group in the mini-book.

Read, read, read!
- ✓ Visit your library or bookstore and help your child find the 100 Great Books for 2nd Graders listed on our poster.

Table of Contents

Editorial Consultant: Mary C. Rose, Orange County Public Schools, Orlando, Florida • **Writers:** Kama Einhorn; Anne Schreiber; Gail Tuchman; Kathryn McKeon **Illustrators:** Valeria Petrone; Greg Paprocki; Jackie Snider **Art Director:** Nancy Sabato **Composition:** Kevin Callahan, BNGO Books **Cover:** Red Herring Design

My 100 Words

Group 1

all	long	slept
drank	man	some
drink	men	take
him	none	took
his	sleep	

Group 2

ask	funny	say
brother	pretty	school
brown	purple	short
child	read	sister
children	said	white

Group 3

both	make	us
but	myself	woman
her	our	women
hers	sang	your
made	sing	

Group 4

cold	large	Sunday
first	Monday	third
Friday	Saturday	Thursday
keep	second	Tuesday
kept	small	Wednesday

Group 5

any	good-bye	thank
best	hello	their
better	help	them
every	many	town
few	please	

Group 6

after	open	when
before	soon	where
here	then	who
how	there	why
now	what	

Group 7

early	more	summer
end	over	under
fall	quiet	wide
fell	spring	winter
into	story	

Drink Up!

Circle everything that you can drink.

Put an X on everything you drank yesterday.

What's your favorite thing to drink?

Verb Time

Verbs are **action** words, like run or jump. Find each verb from the word box in the word search below.

a	q	s	l	e	e	p	a
d	m	p	o	r	v	r	d
s	q	y	a	w	t	y	r
l	u	t	o	o	k	z	i
e	d	m	n	g	t	b	n
p	e	b	d	r	a	n	k
t	i	o	e	p	k	l	m
e	f	r	x	w	e	q	u

Time Travel

It's a time machine!
Write the verbs that describe something
that already happened under **past**.
Write the verbs that describe something happening
right now under **present**.

Word Box

drink   drank   sleep   slept   take   took

past

_____
- - - - - - - - - - - -
_____
- - - - - - - - - - - -
_____
- - - - - - - - - - - -
_____

present

_____
- - - - - - - - - - - -
_____
- - - - - - - - - - - -
_____
- - - - - - - - - - - -
_____

Match It!

Draw a line from each sentence to the picture it matches.

1. The man takes a long drink.

2. The men are standing in line.

3. He **drank** all the milk.

4. This cat likes to sleep in his bed.

5. The girl has long hair.

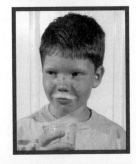

6. The man **ate** some popcorn.

Now try this! Write a sentence using the two blue words from the sentences above.

_____

- - - - - - - - - - - - - - - - - - -

_____

_____

- - - - - - - - - - - - - - - - - - -

_____

Picture This!

Use words from the box to complete the sentences.
Hint: You may have to use capital letters!

Word Box

| some | all | none | long |

_____

1. _____ of the fish are purple.

2. _____ of the starfish are yellow.

3. _____ of the fish have stripes.

4. One of the fish is very _____.

5. This girl wanted to see a jellyfish, but there were _____.

Big News!

Use the words from the box to finish these sentences. Hint: You may have to use capital letters!

_____

A _____ broke a world record yesterday when

he _____ for 20 years. No one had ever _____

for so _____ before.

"I wasn't tired and I couldn't _____, so

I _____ some warm milk," the man, Mr. Rip Van Winkle,

said as photographers _____ pictures. "Then the next

thing I knew, I woke up and everyone was staring at me.

_____ my friends looked different. _____

places in town had changed. Everything was mixed up.

I think I need another nap."

Who's Hiding?

Find all the action words that tell something happening now.
Color all the spaces with those verbs yellow.

Find all the words that tell something has already happened.
Color all the spaces with those verbs red.

Color all the spaces with words that are not verbs green.

Remember: Verbs are action words.

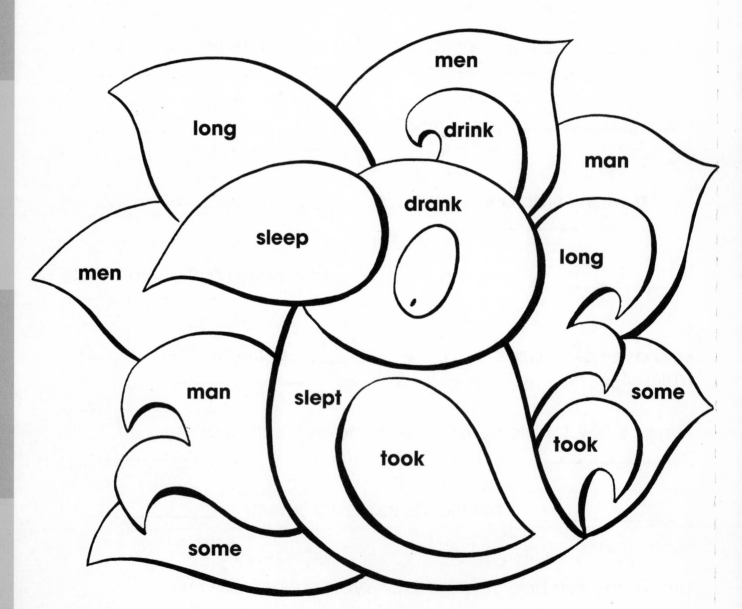

Threes & Fours

Use the words from the box to answer the questions.

Word Box

all	his	men	took	none
him	man	take	long	

_____

Which 4-letter word rhymes with **song**? _____

Which 4-letter word rhymes with **sun**? _____

Which 3-letter word ends with **l** and means **every**? _____

Which 4-letter word starts with **t** and rhymes with **book**? _____

Which 3-letter word starts with **h** and ends with **m**? _____

Which 4-letter word rhymes with **bake**? _____

Which 3-letter word means **more than one man**? _____

Which 3-letter word rhymes with **pan**? _____

Which 3-letter word means **belongs to him**? _____

All Mixed Up

Unscramble the sentences. Write the words in the correct sentence order on the lines. Look at the pictures for clues.

The all man night slept long.

_____

- - - - - - - - - - - - - - - - - -

_____

_____

- - - - - - - - - - - - - - - - - -

_____

The took man candy some.

_____

- - - - - - - - - - - - - - - - - -

_____

_____

- - - - - - - - - - - - - - - - - -

_____

cat the all milk drink The will.

_____

- - - - - - - - - - - - - - - - - -

_____

_____

- - - - - - - - - - - - - - - - - -

_____

All men of the cars have.

_____

- - - - - - - - - - - - - - - - - -

_____

_____

- - - - - - - - - - - - - - - - - -

_____

Mystery Man

Draw a picture to match this description.

The man is short.

His hair is brown.

His hair is not long.

His eyes are blue.

He has some freckles.

All of his clothes are purple!

Now give your mystery man a name.

_____

- -

_____

The Sleepiest Cat

Use the words from the box to finish this poem.

Word Box

sleep   take   all

_____ _____

My cat can _____ _____ day,

_____ _____

She can _____ _____ night,

No matter if it's dark or light.

_____

She always wants to _____ a nap,

Even in my baseball cap!

Now read the poem out loud!

The Vacation

Use the words from the box
to finish these sentences.

_____

I _____ in a funny bed.

_____

We saw _____ beautiful birds

_____

with _____ beaks.

_____

I met _____ other kids.

_____

They were _____ really nice.

_____

We _____ lots of pictures.

_____

I _____ a delicious fruit drink.

Word Group One   15

Word Math

Can you solve these letter math problems? Write the picture name, then add and subtract letters to make a new word.

— sh + sl = _____

— p + m = _____

— b = _____

— t + m = _____

Puzzle Time

Use the words in the box to finish this crossword puzzle.

Word Box

man	drink
men	long
drank	take
sleep	

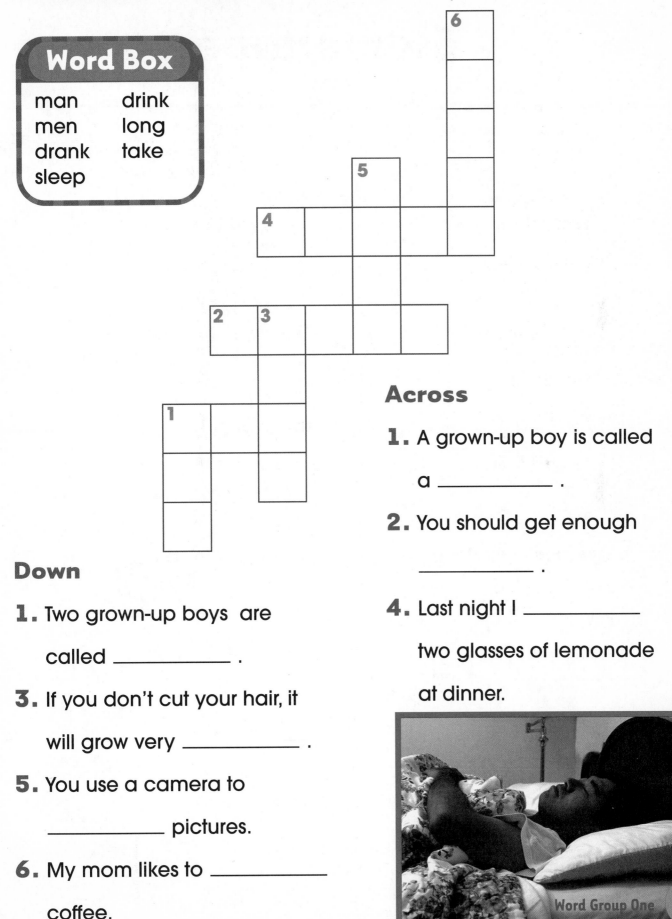

Across

1. A grown-up boy is called a _____ .

2. You should get enough _____ .

4. Last night I _____ two glasses of lemonade at dinner.

Down

1. Two grown-up boys are called _____ .

3. If you don't cut your hair, it will grow very _____ .

5. You use a camera to _____ pictures.

6. My mom likes to _____ coffee.

The Mystery of Elemenopee

In each set of words, the same letter is missing. But is it **l**, **m**, **n**, **o**, or **p**? Write the mystery letter at the end of each set.

1. d r a __ k
   d r i __ k
   m a __   ____
   m e __   ----
The mystery letter is____.

2. h i __
   __ a n
   __ e n   ____
   s o __ e   ----
The mystery letter is____.

3. a __ __
   __ o n g
   s __ e e p   ____
   s __ e p t   ----
The mystery letter is____.

4. s l e e __   ____
   s l e __ t   ----
The mystery letter is____.

5. l __ n g
   n __ n e
   s __ m e   ____
   t __ __ k   ----
The mystery letter is____.

Make Lemonade!

Use the words from the box to finish this delicious recipe for lemonade. Hint: You may need to use capital letters.

Word Box

| take | some | long | drink | all |

Lemonade

_____ _____

1. _____ _____ lemons and slice them.

2. Squeeze _____ the juice from the lemons into a pitcher.

3. Add water and _____ sugar.

4. Stir with a _____ wooden spoon.

5. _____ it up!

A New Puppy

Circle the word that finishes each sentence.

Maria has a new puppy! She will feed (him, his).

She will play with (his, him).

She will brush (him, his) fur.

Maria will (drink, take) her puppy to the vet.

She will make sure he gets (some, all) (him, his) shots.

She will give (him, his) water to (drink, take).

She will let him get (some, all) sleep.

She will walk (him, his) every day.

Some, All, or None?

Use **Some**, **All**, or **None** to finish each sentence about your friends and family.

1. _____ of the kids in my class have freckles.

2. _____ of the kids in my class ride their bikes to school.

3. _____ of the people in my family like to play checkers.

4. _____ of the people in my family have blond hair.

5. _____ of my friends have blue eyes.

6. _____ of my friends like to play outside.

7. _____ of my friends like pizza.

8. _____ of my friends have curly hair.

Sort It Out!

Write each word from the word box in the correct group.

Word Box

drank	take
some	slept
sleep	drink
took	none
all	

Action Words (Verbs)

_____   _____

- - - - - - - - - - - -   - - - - - - - - - - - -

_____   _____

_____   _____

- - - - - - - - - - - -   - - - - - - - - - - - -

_____   _____

_____   _____

- - - - - - - - - - - -   - - - - - - - - - - - -

_____   _____

Words That Tell How Much

_____

- - - - - - - - - - - -

_____

_____

- - - - - - - - - - - -

_____

_____

- - - - - - - - - - - -

What Happened?

Read the story and circle the right answers.

> Last night Shelly went to sleep and had a weird dream. She dreamed all of the kids in her class were wearing pajamas. Some of the kids had on cowboy hats, too! Her teacher had all his clothes on inside out.
>
> The class went to lunch and everyone drank five strawberry milkshakes. Shelly didn't want to drink one, because she doesn't like strawberry. She drank it anyway — and it tasted like chocolate! "Weird!" said Shelly when she finally woke up.

1. Shelly had a weird dream:
   a. last night
   b. a week ago
   c. when she took a nap during the day

2. The kids in school wore:
   a. party hats and shoes
   b. pajamas and cowboy hats
   c. inside-out clothes

3. What happened at lunch?
   a. the kids drank five milkshakes
   b. the kids drank milk
   c. the teacher gave a test

4. What was strange about Shelly's teacher?
   a. he was standing on his head
   b. his clothes were backwards
   c. his clothes were inside out

5. What was strange about the milkshake Shelly drank?
   a. it was strawberry, but it tasted like chocolate
   b. it was chocolate, but it tasted like strawberry
   c. it tasted like milk

A-maze-ing!

Some of the sentences below are true. Some are false. To get through the maze, you have to draw a line through all seven true sentences. Don't get tricked!

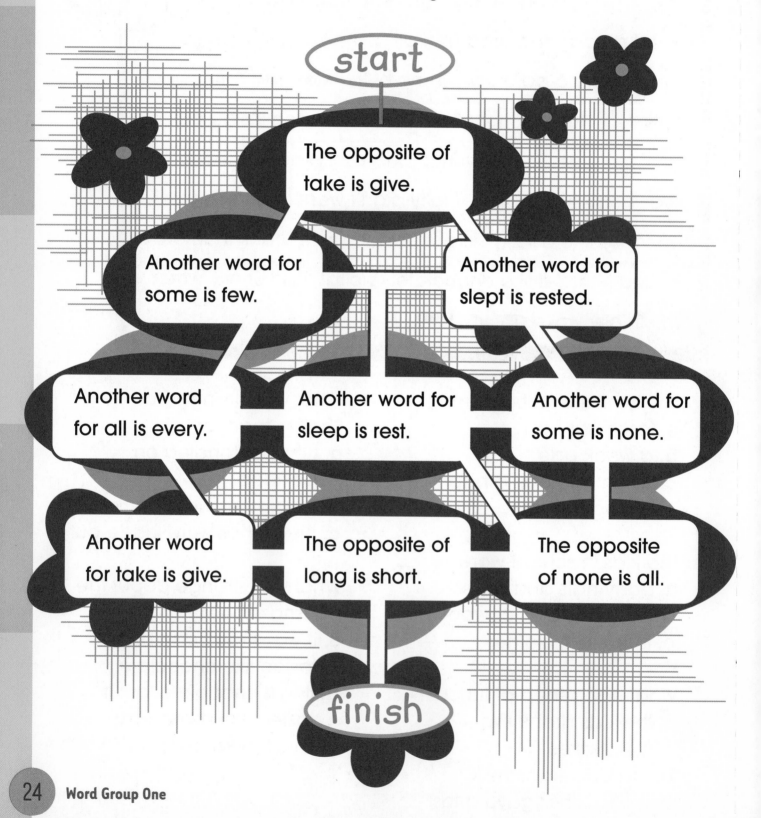

Flower Power

Read the words on the petals. In the center of each flower,
write the word that rhymes with all the petal words.
Choose from the words in the box.

Word Box

all   drank   none   took

Words Within Words

There are smaller words hiding in each of these words.
Can you find them? Write them on the lines.

1. drink ___in___ _____ _____

2. none _____ _____ _____

3. some _____ _____

4. his _____ _____

5. man _____ _____

Tongue Twisters

Read this tongue twister out loud five times fast.

David Drake and his dad drank a delicious drink.

Draw a picture to go with it!

Now try this one! Say this tongue twister out loud:

One man, many men.

Draw a picture that shows the difference between **man** and **men**.

Many Men

What do you notice about these people? Write words from the box to complete the sentences.

Word Box

All   Some   None

_____

- - - - - - - - - - -

1. _____ of the people are men.

_____

- - - - - - - - - - - - -

2. _____ of the men are wearing hats.

_____

- - - - - - - - - - - - -

3. _____ of the men have red hair.

_____

- - - - - - - - - - - - -

4. _____ of the men have brown eyes.

_____

- - - - - - - - - - - - -

5. _____ of the men are wearing ties.

_____

- - - - - - - - - - - - -

6. _____ of the men look like they need some sleep.

Buggy Riddles

Word Box

his	slept	long
all	drink	Take

Finish the riddles. Then
draw lines to their answers! You can use words more than once.

_____

- - - - - - - -

A boy caught us in _____ jar.

_____

- - - - - - - - -

We _____ twinkle like baby stars.

I can play a funny trick.

_____

- - - - - - - - - - -

_____ another look, you'll see:

_____

- - - - - - - - - - -

I'm a _____ walking stick!

_____

- - - - - - - - -

I _____ in a cocoon,

_____

- - - - - - - -

_____ warm and dark

_____

- - - - - - - - -

Now I _____ nectar,

I'm a Monarch.

Line Up!

Fill in the blanks with letters to complete the words.
Hint: The words in the box will help you.

Word Box

drank   him   men   drink   none

Now write the letters in the red boxes to answer this riddle.

Where do mermaids go to see the movies?

___ ___ ___ ___   ___ ___

- - - - - - - - - - - - - - - - - - -   - - - - - - - -

The ___ ___ ___ ___ — ___ ___!

The Alphabet Caterpillar

Put these words in ABC order:
slept, man, long, some, drink, men, him, none, take, his, sleep

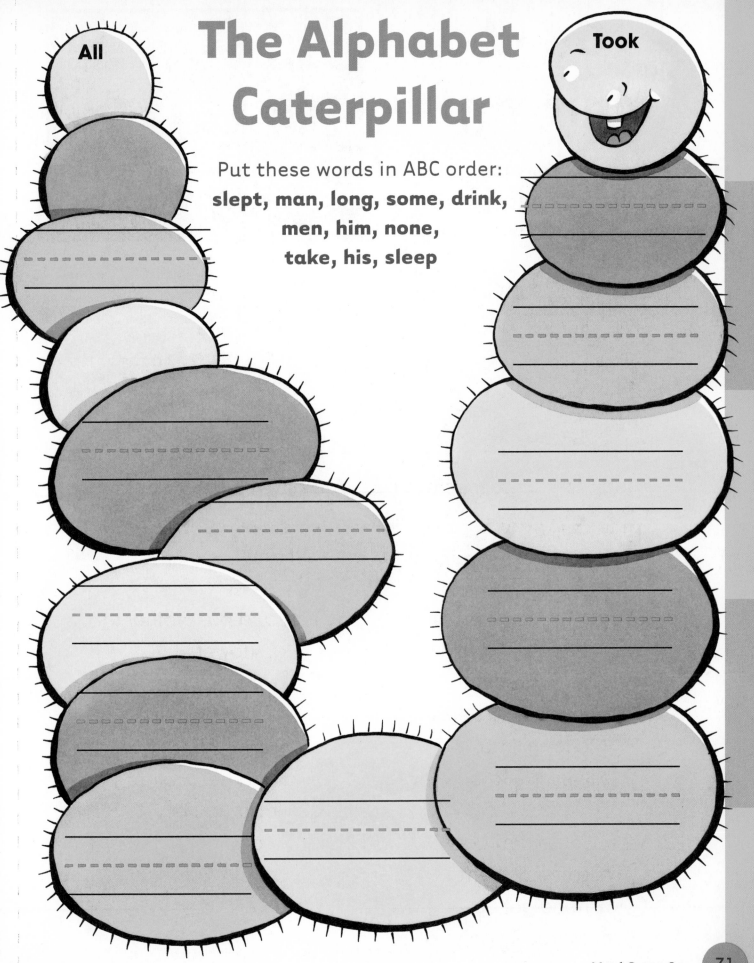

All

Took

Good Morning!

Read the story below. Then finish the sentences by filling in the correct circle.

My name is Tina. At my house, we all like to sleep a long time. If my family slept as long as we like, none of us would be on time. That is why we have an alarm clock. When it goes off, some of us get up. My brother stays in his bed. I go in to wake him. We take showers. We eat and drink some milk. Then my dad drives to work with the man next door. My mom takes the train. My brother and I take the bus to school.

1. The family needs an alarm clock because
- ○ a. they are cold.
- ○ b. they like to sleep a long time.
- ○ c. they like to eat.

2. When the alarm goes off
- ○ a. some of them get up.
- ○ b. none get up.
- ○ c. everbody gets up.

3. Tina and her brother take
- ○ a. showers.
- ○ b. baths.
- ○ c. alarm clocks.

4. Tina and her brother go to school by
- ○ a. car
- ○ b. train
- ○ c. bus

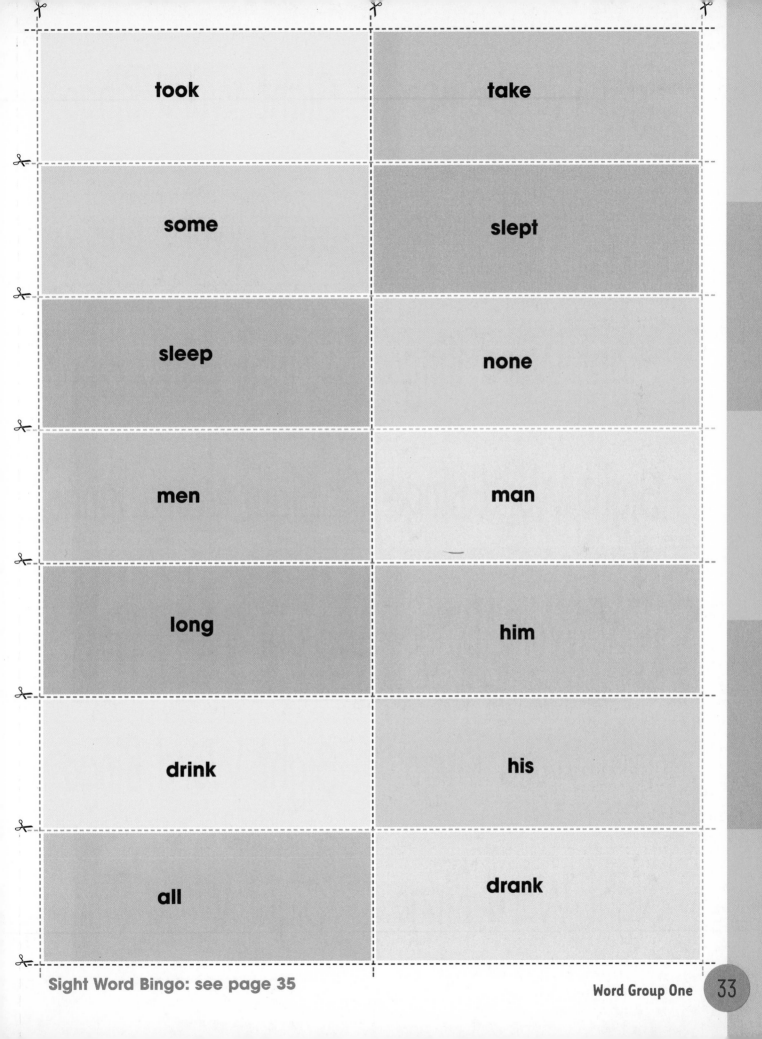

took

take

some

slept

sleep

men

man

long

him

drink

his

all

drank

Sight Word Bingo

Sight Word Bingo

Sight Word Bingo

Sight Word Bingo

Sight Word Bingo

Sight Word Bingo

Sight Word Bingo

Sight Word Bingo

Sight Word Bingo

Sight Word Bingo

Sight Word Bingo

Sight Word Bingo

Sight Word Bingo

Sight Word Bingo

Sight Word Bingo: see page 35

Sight Word Bingo

You'll Need:

- counters (for example: chips, coins, or dried beans)
- paper and pencil for each player

How To Play:

1. On paper, make a board like the one shown below.

2. Cut apart the 14 word cards on page 33 on the dotted lines.

3. Spread them out in front of the players. Each player writes the words in any order on his or her paper board. Use some words twice so that each of the 25 game board squares has a word in it. (Make sure that each player's board is different).

4. The caller gathers the cards, mixes them up, and reads them aloud, one at a time. Players mark the matching squares with an X. The first player to get 5 words in a row calls bingo! Remember: This can mean 5 down, across, or diagonal.

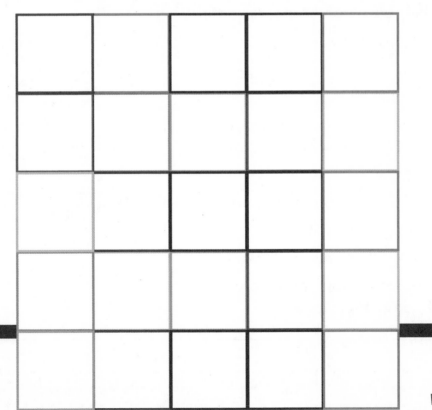

Word Group 1 Answer Key

4 circle milk, juice box, soda, water; answers will vary

5 see right

6 **past**: drank; slept; took **present**: drink; sleep; take

7 draw lines to match text to photos; sentences will vary

8 1. None; 2. All; 3. Some; 4. long; 5. none

9 man; slept; slept; long; sleep; drank; took; All; Some

10 bird

11 long; none; all; took; him; take; men; man; his

12 The man slept all night long. The cat will drink all the milk. The man took some candy. All of the men have cars.

13 answers will vary

14 sleep; all; sleep; all; take

15 slept; some; long; some, all; took; drank

16 sleep; man; all; men

17 **Down:** 1. men; 3. long; 5. take; 6. drink **Across:** 1. man; 2. sleep; 4. drank

18 1. n; 2. m; 3. l; 4. p; 5. o

19 1. Take, some; 2. all; 3. some; 4. long; 5. Drink

20 circle: him; him; his; take; all, his; him, drink; some; him

21 answers will vary

22 **Action words:** drank; sleep; take; took; slept; drink **Words that tell how much:** some; all; none

23 1. a; 2. b; 3. a; 4. c; 5. a

24 see right

25 none; took; drank; all

26 choose from 1. in, ink, rink, rind, kind, din, kin, rid, kid; 2. no, on, one; 3. so, me; 4. hi, is; 5. am, a, an

27 pictures will vary

28 1. All; 2. All; 3. Some; 4. Some; 5. None; 6. Some

29 his, all; Take, long; slept, all, drink

30 drank; him; men; drink; none; dive-in

31 drink; him; his; long; man; men; none; sleep; slept; some; take; took

32 1. b; 2. a; 3. a; 4. c

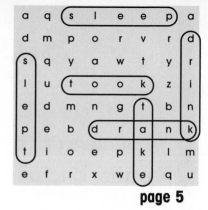

page 5

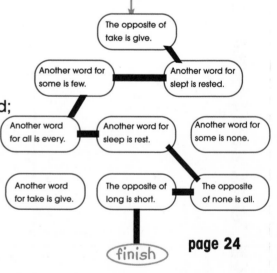

page 24

It was a truck. The man driving it waved.
Some men jumped off. They dug through all
the snow that blocked the sidewalk. Now Jake
and Maria could get through!

"Thanks!" said Jake to the men.

"Would you like some hot chocolate?"
Maria asked.

None of the men said no!

fold & assemble

The Snow Diggers

Written by Anne Schreiber
Illustrated by Greg Paprocki

Scholastic 100 Words Kids Need
to Read by 2nd Grade, Word Group 1

Maria had an idea. She called Jake and told him her plan.

"We can dig a tunnel!" she told him.

Jake and Maria went outside. They began to dig. They each dug all the way to the street. And then they stopped.

"I can't dig through!" Maria called from her side.

"What's that sound?" Jake called from his side.

7

Jake and Maria were best friends. Some days they played inside. Some days they played outside. Jake and Maria played together all year long.

2

That night, it snowed, snowed, snowed, snowed!

The next day, there was snow on the street. There was snow on the sidewalk. There was so much snow Jake and Maria could not go outside.

One hot summer day, Jake and Maria set up a lemonade stand.

"Let's drink some of our lemonade," said Maria.

"Okay," said Jake.

They drank the lemonade until it was all gone.

"We didn't make much money," said Maria.

"But we had fun," said Jake.

Jake and Maria liked winter best of all. They loved to play in the snow. One day, they made a snowman.

Jake took off his scarf.

"Take this," he told Maria. "Put it around our snowman."

Now Jake was cold. He and Maria went inside. They drank hot chocolate.

One night in the fall, Jake and Maria did not go to sleep. They stayed up late. They sat outside in the dark. Maria held a flashlight.

Jake read scary stories from a book.

"That's spooky!" said Maria.

"I'm scared!" said Jake.

"Time for bed!" their mothers called. Jake and Maria slept with their lights on all night long!

Word Search

Find each of these words in the word search: **ask**, **child**, **funny**, **read**, **said**, **school**, **short**, **children**.

s	f	u	n	n	y	p	c
d	a	p	o	r	v	r	h
s	q	i	a	s	k	c	i
h	u	t	d	c	k	h	l
o	d	m	n	h	t	i	d
r	e	a	d	o	u	l	r
t	i	o	e	o	k	d	e
e	f	r	x	l	y	q	n

The Right Word

Fill in the blanks with the right words from the box.

Word Box

brother	brown	pretty	purple	said
say	short	sister	white	

1. I got my hair cut and now it's _____.

2. My dog is black with _____ and _____

   spots.

3. My mom _____ I could go to the movies.

4. This is Patty and this is Pete. They are _____

   and _____ .

5. My mom said the flowers I gave her are _____ .

6. Remember to _____ please and thank you.

7. Violets are _____ .

My Trip

Look at these pictures from Samantha's vacation! Then use the words in the box to finish the sentences.

Word Box

pretty long brother brown
funny sister white

Our family went to London, England.

_____ _____

My _____ and _____

and I sat together on the plane.

_____

It was a _____ flight.

_____

We flew through _____ clouds.

_____

We saw _____ gardens.

_____

We went to see a _____ play.
We laughed and laughed!

_____

Our hotel was made of _____
brick.

What Color?

Color the spaces the color they are labeled.

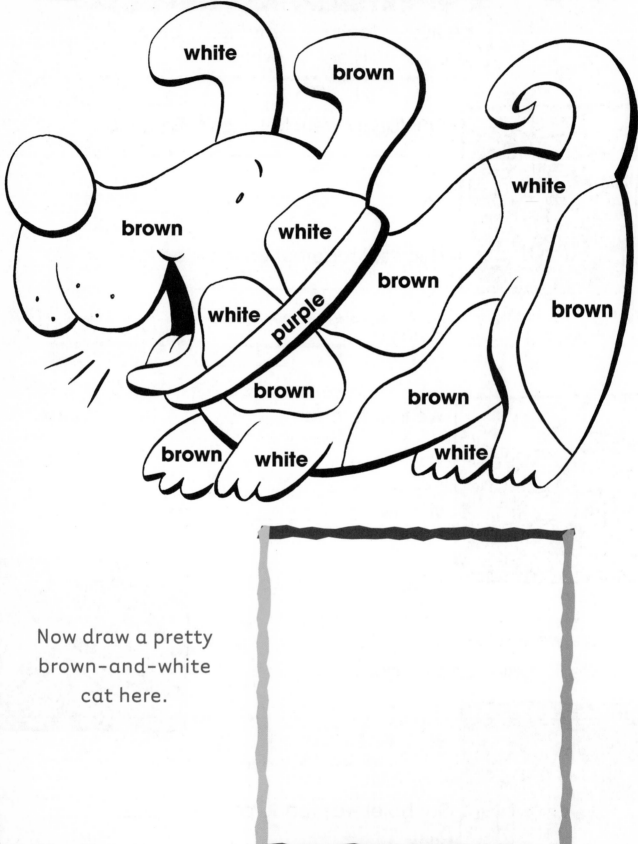

Now draw a pretty brown-and-white cat here.

Family Tree

Look at this family tree. Then use the words in the box to fill in the blanks.

The Garcia Family

Word Box

brother	child
sister	children

Carlos, age 8   Maria, age 6

1. These parents have two _____ .

2. Their older _____ is a boy.

3. Their younger _____ is a girl.

4. Carlos is Maria's _____ .

5. Maria is Carlos's _____ .

Picture Day

Fill in the blanks with the words from the box.

This is my class photo.

_____

----

1. These are all the _____ in the class.
   _____

   - - - - - - - - - - - - - - - -

2. One _____ is wearing a polka-dot shirt.
   _____

   - - - - - - - - - - - - - - - -

3. My teacher is wearing a _____
   _____

   - - - - - - - - - - - - -

   _____ sweater.
   _____

   - - - - - - - - - - - - - - - - -

4. Two of the _____ in the front row
   _____

   - - - - - - - - - - - - - -

   have _____ hair.
   _____

   - - - - - - - - - - - - - -

5. One _____ is wearing a shirt with
   _____   _____

   - - - - - - - - - - -   - - - - - - - - - - -

   _____ and _____ stripes.

What's What?

Draw a line from each sentence to the picture it matches.

Her shirt is blue and red.

The purple flower is pretty.

These children like to read.

The child heard a funny joke.

This is a school.

They are sister and brother.

Sort It Out!

Write each word from the word box where it belongs.

Word Box

ask	children	read	short
brown	funny	said	sister
brother	~~pretty~~	~~say~~	white
~~child~~	purple	school	

NOUNS
(naming words)

child

ADJECTIVES
(describing words)

pretty

VERBS
(action words)

say

Say It Fast!

Finish these tongue twisters with words from the box. Then say them out loud as fast as you can!

Word Box

brown   brother
pretty   purple

_____

Bonny's _____ -eyed

_____

_____ baked brownies.

_____

Penny petted two _____

_____

_____ puppies.

Now make up your own tongue twister with some of these words.

Word Box

| said | school | sister | slept |
| say | short | sleep | some |

_____

_____

_____

_____

Different Sorts of Short

Draw lines between the sentences and the pictures they describe.

I love strawberry shortcake.

I play shortstop on my baseball team.

I took a shortcut home through my friend's backyard.

In the summer, I always wear shorts.

The opposite of tall is short.

Word Safari

Use the words from the box to answer these questions.

Word Box

brown	funny	school	white
child	pretty	sister	

1. What 5-letter word ends in **e** and is an adjective? _____

2. What 6-letter word starts with **s** and rhymes _____

with **Mr.**? _____

3. What 6-letter word starts with the same sound as **prince** and _____

is the opposite of **ugly**? _____

4. What 6-letter word starts with the same sound as the _____

word **scoop**? _____

5. What 5-letter word starts with **br-** and rhymes with **gown**? _____

6. What 5-letter word is an adjective ending in **y**? _____

7. What 5-letter word starts with the same sound as **chair** _____

and ends in **d**? _____

Family Picture

Draw this family's picture with crayons or markers.
Read the descriptions first.

There are three children in the family. One child is a boy. The other two children are girls. The sisters both wear dresses. One sister has short red hair, the other has long blonde hair. Their brother has short brown hair.

Now give this family a last name.

_____

The _____ Family

Which White?

Use the word **white** to finish the sentences. Hint: You may need to use a capital W sometimes.

A beluga lives in the ocean, and is also

_____

- - - - - - - - - - - - - - - - - - - -

called a _____ whale.

_____

- - - - - - - - - - - - - - - - - - - -

_____ and red makes pink.

_____

- - - - - - - - - - - - - - - - - -

My favorite fairy tale is Snow _____

and the Seven Dwarves.

_____

- - - - - - - - - - - - - - - -

The president lives in the _____ House.

Bring in the Brown!

Read the sentences and chose
a word from the box
to complete them.

Word Box

brown bag	brown belt
brown bear	brownies
brown bread	brown sugar

_____ _____

- -

1. Our teacher told us to bring a _____ _____

   lunch on the field trip.

2. Before I get my black belt in Karate, I have to get

   _____ _____

   -

   my _____ _____ .

   _____

   - - - - - - - - - - - - - - - -

3. Cookies and _____ are my favorite treats.

   _____ _____

   -

4. The recipe calls for _____ _____ .

   _____ _____

   -

5. I saw a _____ _____ in the woods.

   _____ _____

   -

6. Would you like white bread or _____ _____ ?

Solve the Riddle

Choose the best words from the box to fill in the blanks.

Word Box

~~brown~~	white	purple	~~pretty~~	children
brother	sister	say	read	

b r o w n

p r e t t y

Now look at the letters in the red boxes.
They spell the answer to this riddle:

What's black and white and read all over?

_____

- -

A _____ !

Rhyming Starfish

In the center of each starfish,
write the word that rhymes with
all the words on its arms.
Choose from the words in the box.

sunny

runny

_____

bunny

honey

money

spool

rule

_____

pool

fool

bright

bite

_____

kite

night

might

cool

thread

_____

red

head

bed

fed

Purple Cow

Read this poem. Then write one of your own below,
choosing from the words in the box.

I saw a pretty purple cow.
I never thought I'd see one.
It was a funny thing to see,
And I'd rather see, than be, one!

Word Box

pretty   brown   white   purple   funny   short   long

_____ _____

- -

I saw a _____ _____ .
name of animal

I never thought I'd see one.

It was a funny thing to see,

And I'd rather see, than be, one!

Now illustrate your poem.

Rainbow Math

Use the words from the box to do the color math.
Then try it yourself by coloring in the blank crayon.

Word Box

green	red	yellow
orange	purple	blue

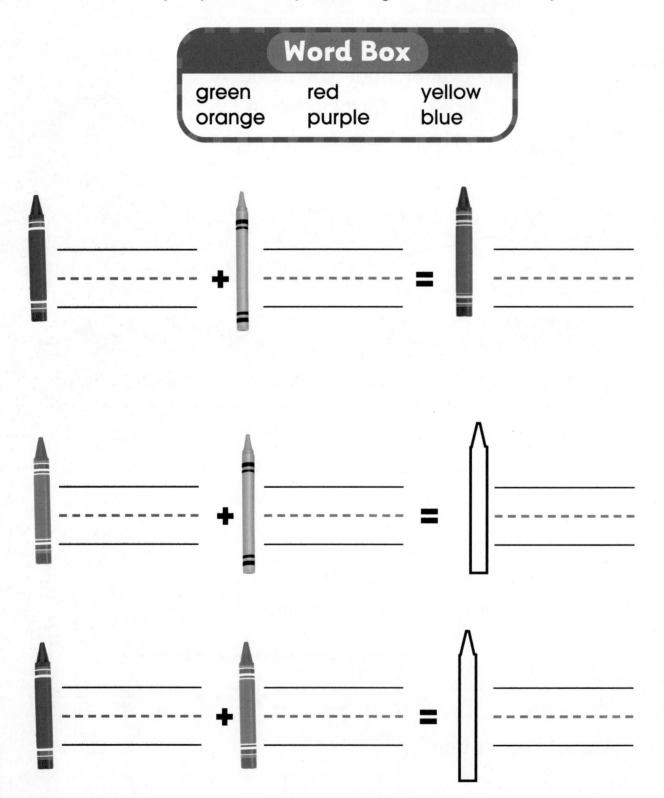

The Mystery Color

Draw lines to match the riddles to their answers.
Then write the color name on the line.

Ask me what I'm made of

and I'll say red and blue.

You know I'm the color of violets, too.
_____

- - - - - - - - - - - - - - -

What color am I? _____

Everyone has me in their eyes,
But you can also find me in cloudy skies.
_____

- - - - - - - - - - - - - - -

What color am I? _____

I'm the color of bark and dirt,
And chocolate pudding for dessert.
_____

- - - - - - - - - - - - - - -

What color am I? _____

Alphabet Staircase

Bedtime! Put these words on the stairs in
ABC order. Start at the bottom and
climb up to your nice,
comfy bed!

Word Box

ask	funny	said
pretty	brother	
white	child	

School Shopping

Write words from the box
to complete the sentences.

Word Box

purple	long
white	school
short	brown

_____

1. I went _____ shopping.

_____

2. I got a _____ scarf.

3. My mom bought me a pair of

_____

_____ shoes.

_____

4. I bought two _____ notebooks.

_____

5. I got two _____ sleeved shirts.

_____

6. I got three _____ sleeved shirts.

Ha-Ha! Use the words from the box to finish the riddles.

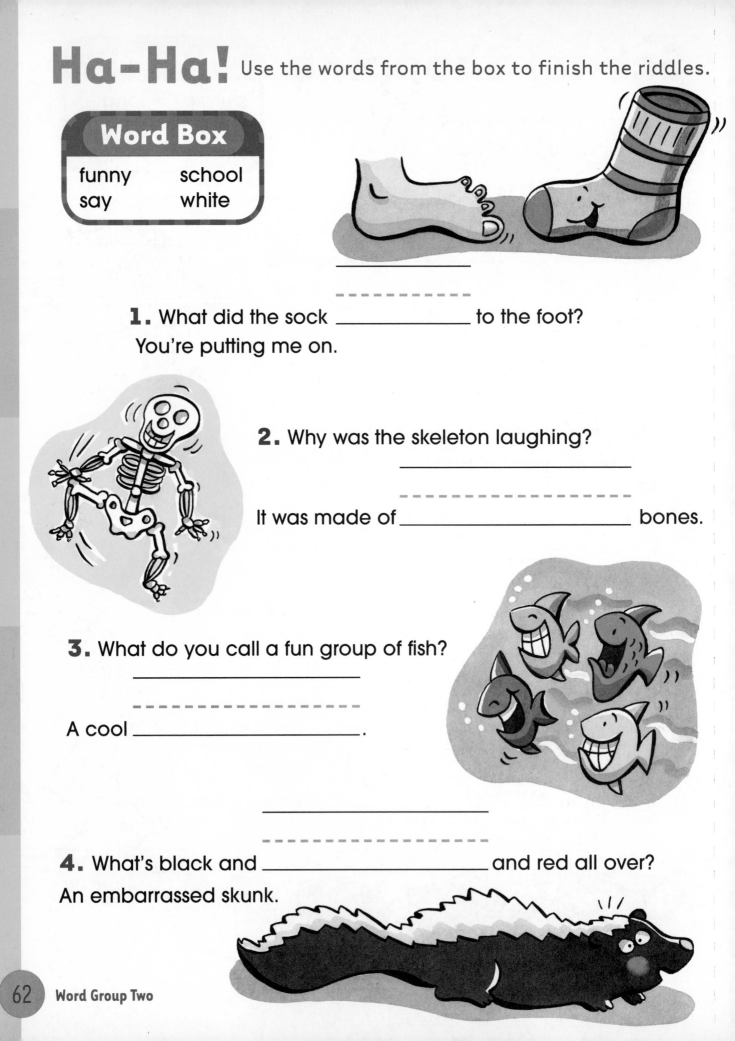

Word Box

funny	school
say	white

_____

- - - - - - - - - - -

1. What did the sock _____ to the foot?
You're putting me on.

2. Why was the skeleton laughing?

_____

- - - - - - - - - - - - - - - - - - - -

It was made of _____ bones.

3. What do you call a fun group of fish?

_____

- - - - - - - - - - - - - - - - - -

A cool _____.

_____

- - - - - - - - - - - - - - - - - - -

4. What's black and _____ and red all over?
An embarrassed skunk.

Adjective Crossword

Complete the crossword puzzle with the words from the box.

Word Box

purple   white   pretty
brown   short

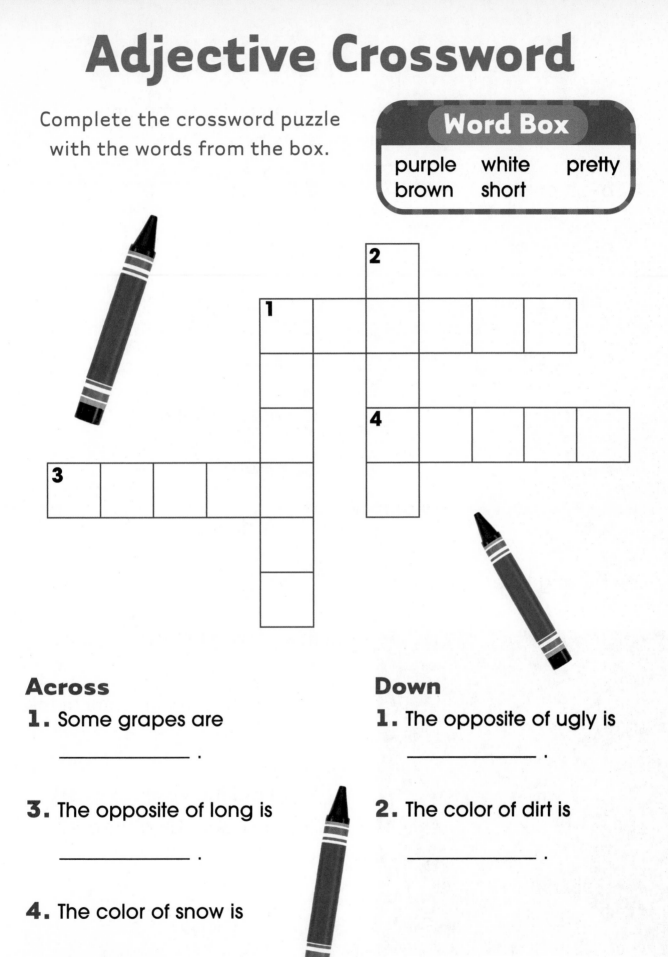

Across

1. Some grapes are

_____ .

3. The opposite of long is

_____ .

4. The color of snow is

_____ .

Down

1. The opposite of ugly is

_____ .

2. The color of dirt is

_____ .

Where's That Letter?

In each set of words, the same letter is missing.
Write the missing letter.

1. b __ own

b __ other

child __ en

pu __ ple

__ ead

sho __ t

siste __   ____

The missing letter is ____.

2. __ sk

re __ d

s __ id

s __ y   ____

The missing letter is ____.

3. brow __

childre __

fu __ __ y   ____

The missing letter is ____.

Write all the missing letters below.
They form the answer to this riddle!

What did the nose do when
it was scared by a sneeze?

____ ____ ____

It ____ ____ ____ !
    1   2   3

Q & A

Draw a line from the question to its answer.

A. Pretty funny, sister!

A. Oh, brother!

Q. There's a town where everyone has a red nose and is very funny. What is it called?

Q. What did one twin say to the other twin when he slipped on a banana peel?

Q. What did one twin say to the other twin when she made a silly face?

A. Clown Town

It All Adds Up

Can you solve these letter math problems? Write the picture name, than add and subtract letters to make a new word.

_____

— c + b =   _ _ _ _ _ _ _ _ _ _ _ _

_____

_ _ _ _ _ _ _ _ _ _ _ _

_____

_____

— h + s =   _ _ _ _ _ _ _ _ _ _ _ _

_____

_ _ _ _ _ _ _ _ _ _ _ _

_____

_____

+ er =   _ _ _ _ _ _ _ _ _ _ _ _

_____

_____

_ _ _ _ _ _ _ _ _ _ _ _

_____

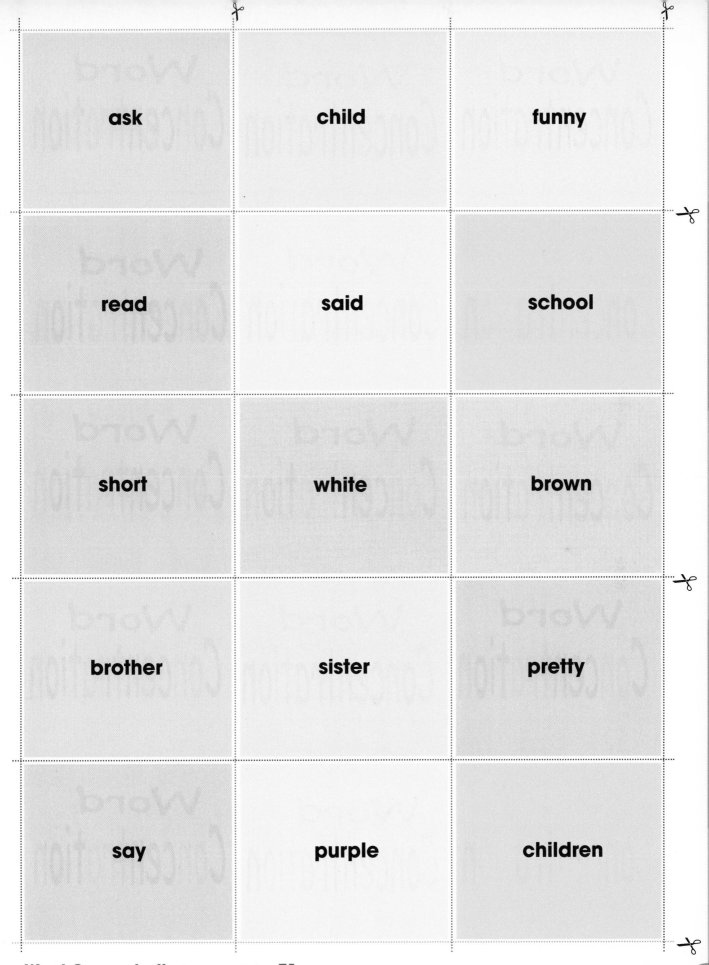

ask	child	funny
read	said	school
short	white	brown
brother	sister	pretty
say	purple	children

Word Concentration: see page 71

Word Concentration	Word Concentration	Word Concentration
Word Concentration	Word Concentration	Word Concentration
Word Concentration	Word Concentration	Word Concentration
Word Concentration	Word Concentration	Word Concentration
Word Concentration	Word Concentration	Word Concentration

Word Concentration: see page 71

Word Concentration

1. Cut apart the 30 cards on pages 67 and 69. Place all cards face down in even rows.
2. Take turns turning over two cards at a time, trying to make a word match.
3. If the words on two cards match, take the cards. If they don't, turn the cards back over.
4. The player with the most cards at the end wins!

Word Concentration
Word Concentration
Word Concentration
Word Concentration
Word Concentration
Word Concentration
Word Concentration
Word Concentration
Word Concentration
Word Concentration
Word Concentration
Word Concentration
Word Concentration

Word Group 2 Answer Key

41 see right

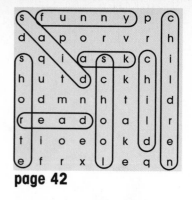

page 42

42 1. short; 2. brown, white; 3. said;
  4. sister; brother, 5. pretty; 6. say; 7. purple

43 brother, sister; long; white; pretty; funny; brown

44 a brown and white puppy with purple collar

45 1. children; 2. child; 3. child; 4. brother; 5. sister

46 1. children; 2. child; 3. pretty, purple; 4. children, short; 5. child, purple, white

47 draw lines connecting text to photos

48 **Adjectives:** brown; funny; purple; short; white;
  Nouns: brother; children; school; sister;
  Verbs: ask; read; said

49 brown; brother; pretty; purple;
  answers will vary

50 draw lines to connect text to pictures

51 1. white; 2. sister; 3. pretty; 4. school;
  5. brown; 6. funny; 7. child

52 answers will vary

53 write white 4 times

54 1. brown bag; 2. brown belt; 3. brownies;
  4 .brown sugar;
  5. brown bear; 6. brown bread

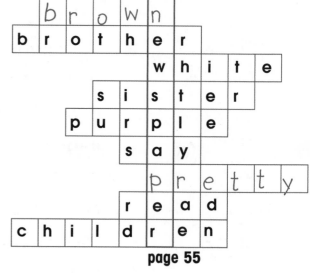

page 55

55 newspaper

56 funny; school; white; said

57 answers will vary

58 blue, yellow, green; red, yellow, orange; blue, red, purple

59 draw lines to match text to pictures; purple; white; brown

60 ask; brother; child; funny; pretty; said; white

61 1. school; 2. long; 3. brown; 4. purple; 5. short; 6. long

62 1. say; 2. funny; 3. school; 4. white

63 **Across:** 1. purple; 3. short; 4. white **Down:** 1. pretty; 2. brown

64 1. r; 2. a; 3. n; ran

65 match questions to answers

66 brown; say; brother

"My rabbits are not pretty funny," she said. "They are just pretty."

"You are still one pretty funny sister," Ben said.

Lizzy just smiled and tapped her purple shoes.

8

---

fold & assemble

Lizzy's Purple Rabbits

Written by Kathryn McKeon
Illustrated by Valeria Petrone

Scholastic 100 Words Kids Need to Read by 2nd Grade, Word Group 2

1

After school, Lizzy walked home with her brother Ben. She gave her brother her picture of the purple rabbits.

"Rabbits are not purple," said Lizzy's brother. "These rabbits look pretty funny."

Ben's little sister Lizzy loved purple. She had a purple dress. She had a purple hat. She even had purple shoes.

"Purple is so pretty," said Lizzy.

Lizzy's teacher looked at the pictures. One picture was not like all of the rest.

"Lizzy," said the teacher. "May I ask you why your rabbits are purple?"

"Purple is so pretty," said Lizzy.

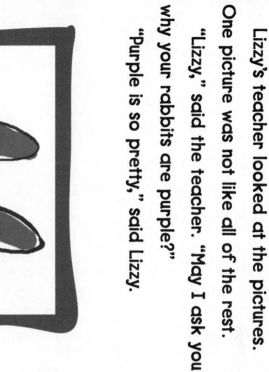

On Monday, Lizzy and her brother went to school. Lizzy wore her purple shoes.

"Children," said Lizzy's teacher. "I will read a short story.

Then each child will draw a picture about the story."

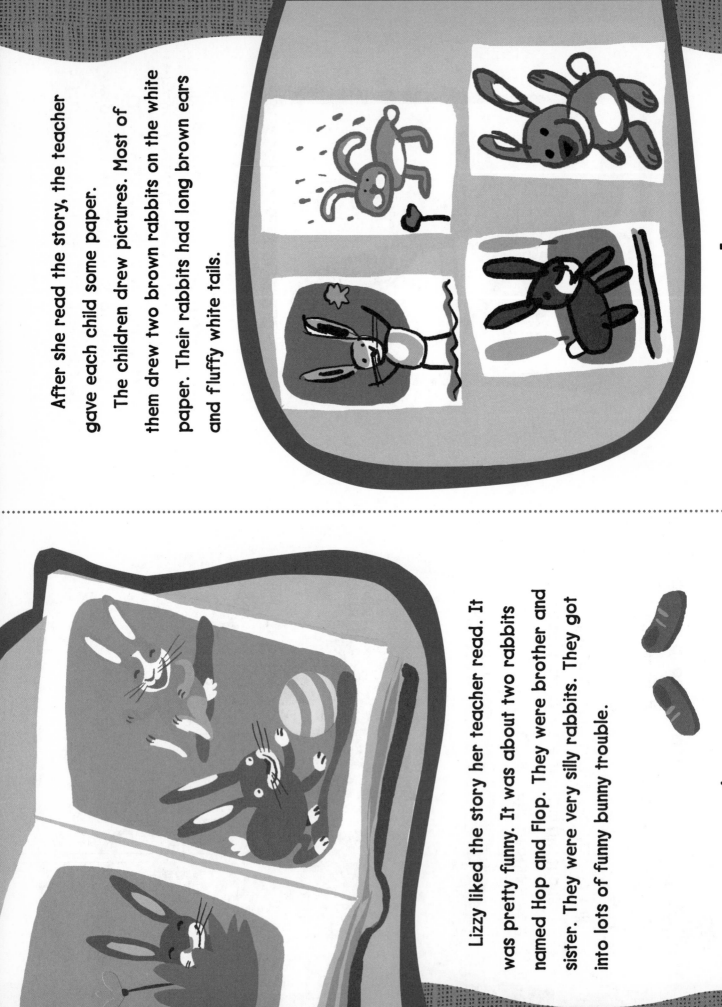

After she read the story, the teacher gave each child some paper.

The children drew pictures. Most of them drew two brown rabbits on the white paper. Their rabbits had long brown ears and fluffy white tails.

5

Lizzy liked the story her teacher read. It was pretty funny. It was about two rabbits named Hop and Flop. They were brother and sister. They were very silly rabbits. They got into lots of funny bunny trouble.

4

When?

Write the verbs that tell about something that already happened in the column labeled **yesterday**. Write the verbs that tell about something happening right now in the column labeled **today**.

Word Box

made   make   sing   sang

yesterday

_____
- - - - - - - - - - - - -
_____
_____
- - - - - - - - - - - - -
_____

today

_____
- - - - - - - - - - - - -
_____
_____
- - - - - - - - - - - - -
_____

Fix It!

The clock is broken. It can't tell what's in the **past** and what's in the **present**! Fix it by unscrambling the words.

_____

kame _____

_____

edam _____

_____

ings _____

_____

nags _____

_____

yas _____

_____

dais _____

Put a ✓ after the **present** tense words.

Twins

Fill in the blanks with words from the box.

Word Box

both   her   hers   our   us   but

_____

We're Tisha and Kisha! We are twins. We _____ have

_____   _____

hats. _____ hats have flowers on them. Both of _____

look the same, _____ we are different people.

Tisha likes apples in _____ cereal. Kisha likes pears

in _____. There's one way we are exactly the same.

We both love each other a lot!

Picture It!

Look at the picture.
Then fill in the blanks
with words from the box.

Word Box

| women | her | but |
| woman | hers | both |

1. All of these people are _____ .

2. One _____ has curly hair. The rest of the
_____
_____ have straight hair.

3. _____ of the _____ on the right are tall.

4. The blond woman has a hat on _____ head.

5. The cat belongs to the woman in the red dress. It is_____.

Possessives

Fill in the blanks for each clue with words from the box. Then complete the puzzle.

Word Box
her   hers   ours   us   your

Across

1. Belongs to her means

it is _____ .

4. Belongs to us means the

same as _____ .

Down

1. Belongs to _____

means it is hers.

2. _____ means

belongs to you.

3. Another word for we is

_____ .

Me, Myself, and I

Fill in the blanks in the poem with the words from the box. Then read it out loud. Hint: You may have to use a capital letter.

Word Box

myself	some	children	our	make	your

Me, Myself, and I

_____ _____

_____ _____ I know very well

_____

are Me, _____ , and I.

_____

_____ times together are really swell—

_____

Me, _____ , and I

It's fun with just the three of us,

I really know who's who.

_____   _____

Let's me, _____ , and I_____ friends

_____

with you, _____ self, and you!

Tongue Twisters

Fill in the blanks to complete the tongue twisters. Then say them out loud as fast as you can!

Word Box

sang   sing   made   myself

_____

Sam _____ six songs,

_____

because he likes to _____ .

_____

I _____ a mess

_____

making muffins by _____ .

Plus or Minus

Can you solve these letter math problems?
Write the picture name, then add and
subtract letters to make a new word.

_____

— k + s = - - - - - - - - - - - - - - - - - -

_____

_____

- -

_____

_____

— n + de = - - - - - - - - - - - - - - - - -

_____

_____

- -

_____

_____

— c + m = - - - - - - - - - - - - - -

_____

_____

- - - - - - - - - - - - - - - - - - - -

_____

_____

— b = - - - - - - - - - -

_____

- - - - - - - - - -

_____

Word Crowd

Write 3 sentences about the photo on this page.
Use one word from the word box in each sentence.

Hidden Words

There are smaller words hiding in each of these words.
Can you find them? Write them on the lines.

Example: d $\widehat{\text{r a n}}$ **k**

your   women   myself

_____   _____   _____

- - - - - - - - - -   - - - - - - - - - -   - - - - - - - - - -

_____   _____   _____

- - - - - - - - - -   - - - - - - - - - -   - - - - - - - - - -

_____   _____   _____

                       - - - - - - - - - -   - - - - - - - - - -

                       _____   _____

Find-a-Word

Fill in the blanks with the right words from the box.

Word Box

both	made
but	make
her	myself
hers	our

1. My brother and I _____ like to ski.

2. I _____ this cake all by _____ !

3. He knows how to _____ pizza.

4. The book belongs to _____ . It is _____ .

5. My favorite flavor is chocolate, _____ my friend's is vanilla.

6. I went on vacation with my family. It was _____ best trip ever!

Word Search

Find all the words from the box in the word search.

Word Box

sing	sang	us	women	woman	your

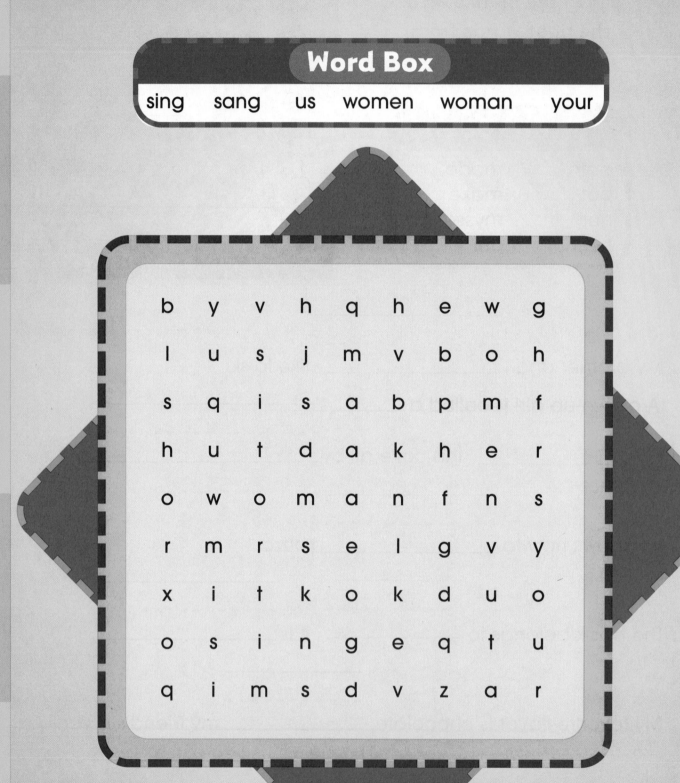

```
b  y  v  h  q  h  e  w  g
l  u  s  j  m  v  b  o  h
s  q  i  s  a  b  p  m  f
h  u  t  d  a  k  h  e  r
o  w  o  m  a  n  f  n  s
r  m  r  s  e  l  g  v  y
x  i  t  k  o  k  d  u  o
o  s  i  n  g  e  q  t  u
q  i  m  s  d  v  z  a  r
```

Find-a-Word

Fill in the blanks with the words from the box.

Word Box

| sing | us | women |
| sang | woman | your |

1. A grown up girl is called a _____ .

2. Two grown up girls are called _____ .

3. Would you like to play with _____?

4. I _____ in the school concert last night.

5. I like to _____ .

6. I like _____ dog. What's his name?

Sort It Out!

Write each word in the word box in the right circle.

Verbs

made

Word Box

her	~~our~~
sing	your
hers	make
~~made~~	sang

Possessives

our

Match Up

Draw a line from each sentence to the picture it matches.

The women like to sing.

Both dogs are black.

She made her own hat.

The woman has short hair.

Out the Door!

Word Box

both	her	sang	your
but	our	sing	

1. Which 3-letter word rhymes with **purr**? _____

2. Which 4-letter word is a past-tense verb ending in **g**? _____

3. Which 3-letter word means **belonging to us**? _____

4. Which 4-letter word rhymes with **bring**? _____

5. Which 3-letter word begins and ends with **consonants** and has a _____

   short u in the middle? _____

6. Which 4-letter word ends with the same _____

   sound as **math**? _____

7. Which 4-letter word rhymes with **pour**? _____

Camp Days

Use the words from the box
to finish the sentences.

Word Box

made	sang	woman	Both
myself	our	her	

I went to camp. I _____ lots of things _____.

_____ of my best friends were at my camp.

We _____ songs around the fire.

_____ song was loud!

The camp swim teacher was a _____.

I liked _____.

Verb Riddles

Finish the riddles using verbs (action words) from the word box.

Word Box

make	made
sang	sing

Birds do this, often in spring.

_____

- - - - - - - - - - - - - - -

I am the verb to _____ .

Doing arts and crafts or baking a cake,

_____

- - - - - - - - - - - - - -

I am the verb to _____ .

I knocked some paints

right off the shelf.   _____

- - - - - - - - - - - - - -

What a mess! (And I _____ it myself!)

The party was a surprise.

I had no clue,   _____

- - - - - - - - - - - - - -

until my friends all _____

"Happy Birthday to you!"

Finish the Joke

Finish the sentences with the words from the boxes.

Word Box

women   both   made   us

Why does the letter **S**

_____

- - - - - - - - -

scare _____ ?

_____

- - - - - - - - - - - - - - - -

Because it _____

our ice cream scream!

What do you call two

_____

- -

wicked old _____

_____

- - - - - - - - - - - - - - - -

who _____ live on

a beach?

Sandwitches!

What's So Funny?

Fill in the boxes with the words that fit best.
Choose from the words in the box. Then answer the riddle
with the words in the red boxes.

Word Box

~~myself~~   our   make   both   woman   women

m y s e l f

l

k

What do you call a funny book about eggs?

_____   _____

_ _ _ _ _ _ _ _ _ _ _ _ _   _ _ _ _ _ _ _ _ _ _ _ _ _

A _____   _____.

Mystery Letter

In each set of words, the same letter is missing.
Write the mystery letter.

1. h __ r

h __ rs

mad __

mys __ lf

wom __ n   ____

                  - - - -

The mystery letter is ____ .

2. __ oth

__ ut   ____

                        - - - -

The mystery letter is ____ .

4. m __ de

m __ ke

s __ ng

wom __ n   ____

                  - - - -

The mystery letter is ____ .

3. he __

he __ s

you __   ____

                  - - - -

The mystery letter is ____ .

Fill in the blanks with the mystery letters,
in order, to read the answer to the question:

If a dictionary goes from A to Z,
what goes from Z to A?

_____ _____ _____ _____

- - - - - - - - - - - - - -

A z _____ !

A-maze-ing!

Draw a line through the path of boxes that contain true sentences. The correct path takes you through seven boxes.

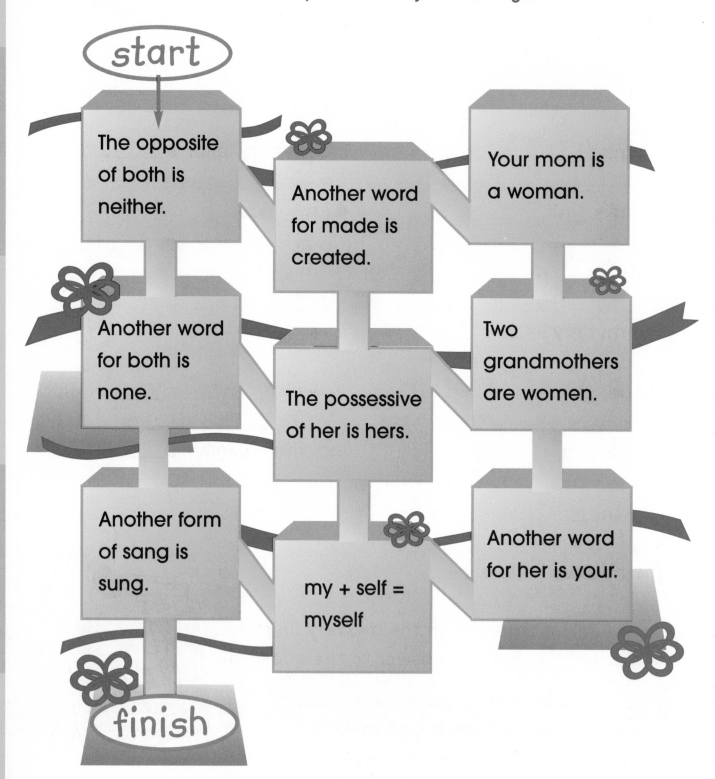

start

The opposite of both is neither.

Another word for made is created.

Your mom is a woman.

Another word for both is none.

The possessive of her is hers.

Two grandmothers are women.

Another form of sang is sung.

my + self = myself

Another word for her is your.

finish

Alphabet Path

Put these words in ABC order on the path.
Start at the beginning of the path and go all the way to the end!

Word Box

make	myself	~~but~~	her	our	woman
~~both~~	sang	women	made	us	your

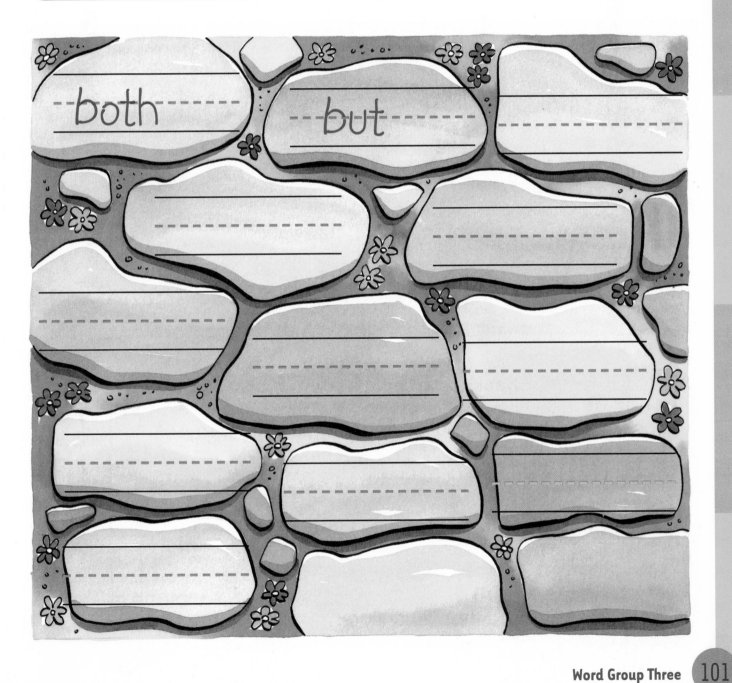

both

but

All About Me

Tell about yourself.
Then draw yourself in the frame.

_____

My name is _____ .

I am _____ years old.

Check **yes** or **no** after each sentence.

	yes	no
I can make a peanut butter and jelly sandwich myself.	☐	☐
My teacher is a woman.	☐	☐
I like both chocolate and vanilla ice cream.	☐	☐
I like to sing.	☐	☐
Our class has more than 20 children.	☐	☐

Word Blocks

Use the words from the word box to finish the blocks.

Word Box

| ~~both~~ | her | hers | make | sang |
| but | our | made | his | sing |

Upside-Down Cake

Use the words in the box to complete the sentences.

Word Box

make	our	but
both	your	Sing

_____

Would you like to learn how to _____ a special cake?

Here's how:

_____

Mix all the ingredients together and bake the cake, _____

_____

be careful not to bake it for too long. _____ or whistle

_____

while you wait. It makes the time go faster. Use _____

oven mitts to take the cake out of the oven. Let it cool and frost it.

_____

Eat it standing on _____ head, and it will be upside-down

_____

cake! Share it with _____ friends!

both

but

her

hers

made

make

your

myself

our

sang

sing

us

woman

women

Flash!   Flash!

Flash!   Flash!

Flash!   Flash!

Flash!   Flash!

Flash!   Flash!

Flash!   Flash!

Flash!   Flash!

Flash! See page 107.

Flash!

Play this game with a friend.

1. Cut apart the 14 cards on page 105. Put them in a pile. One player takes a card and does not show it to the other.

2. The player with the card begins to slowly spell out the word on the card. As quickly as possible, the other player has to say the word being spelled.

3. If he or she guesses correctly before the speller finishes spelling the word, he or she keeps the card. If not, the speller keeps the card. The player with the most cards at the end wins.

Word Group 3 Answer Key

77 **yesterday:** made; sang **today:** make; sing

78 make, made; sing, sang; say, said; put a ✓ after: make; sing; say

79 sing; made; her; your

80 make; makeup; make believe; make it; answers will vary

81 both; Our; us; but; her; hers

82 1. women; 2. woman, women; 3. Both, women; 4. her; 5. hers

83 **Across:** 1. hers; 4. our **Down:** 1. her; 2. your; 3. us

84 Some, children; myself; Our; myself; myself, make; your

85 sang, sing; made, myself

86 sing; made; make; us

87 answers will vary

88 you, our; me, men; my, self, elf

89 1. both; 2. made, myself; 3. make; 4. her, hers; 5. but; 6. our

90 see right

91 1. woman; 2. women; 3. us; 4. sang; 5. sing; 6. your

92 **verbs:** sing; make; sang
possessives: her; hers; your

93 match text to photos

94 1. her; 2. sang; 3. our; 4. sing; 5. but; 6. both; 7. your

95 made; myself; Both; sang; Our; woman; her

96 sing; make; made; sang

97 us; made; women; both

98 see right; A yolk book

99 1. e; 2. b; 3. r; 4. a; zebra

100 see right

101 both; but; her; made; make; myself; our; sang; us; woman; women; your

102 answers will vary

103 see right

104 make; but; sing; your; your; your

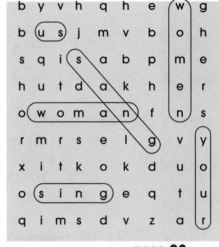

page 90

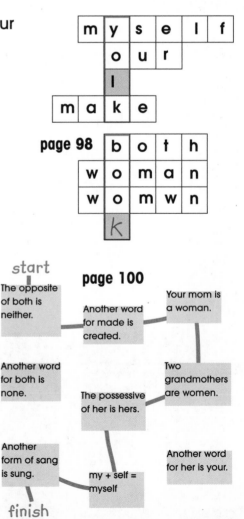

page 98

page 100

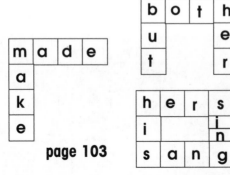

page 103

I sang high.
My friends sang low.
The funny woman sang fast.
The pretty woman sang slow.
We sang song after song, after song,
as our bus just hummed along.

8

fold & assemble

1

BUS SONGS

Written by Gail Tuchman
Illustrated by Jackie Snider

Scholastic 100 Words Kids Need
to Read by 2nd Grade, Word Group 3

I made up a funny song
and sang it on the bus.
All my friends sang along
and the women sang with us.

7

A funny woman sang on the bus.
I liked her funny song.
She sang about six sleepy cats,
and asked us to sing along.

2

6

"Your songs are good," I said to them.
"Singing them is fun.
"But I want to try a song myself.
"It's my turn to make up one."

3

A pretty woman sang on the bus.
I liked her pretty song.
Hers was about blue birds.
She asked us to sing along.

The Right Word

Fill in the blanks with the right words from the box. Hint: You may need to use capital letters.

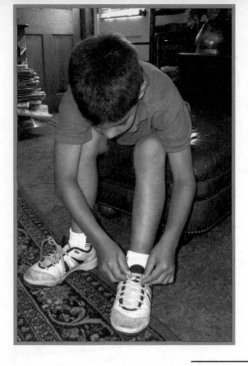

Word Box

cold	keep	large	small
first	kept	second	third

_____

My bare feet are _____ .

_____ , I put on my socks. _____ , I

put on my shoes. _____ , I tie the laces.

When I was little, it took me a while to learn to tie my shoes,

but I _____ trying.

My feet are _____ , but my dad's feet

are _____ .

This week I'll _____ my room clean. I'll put all my shoes

in the closet!

Compared To . . .

bee   cat   mouse   elephant   dinosaur   rhino   flea

Write **large** or **small** on each line.

_____

1. Next to a bumblebee, a cat looks _____ .

2. Next to a cat, a mouse looks _____ .

3. Next to a mouse, an elephant looks _____ .

4. Next to an elephant, a dinosaur looks _____ .

5. Next to a dinosaur, a rhino looks _____ .

6. Next to a rhino, a flea looks _____ .

A Busy Week

Monday	soccer practice 4pm
	Mom's birthday dinner 6 pm
Tuesday	dance lessons
Wednesday	practice piano
Thursday	dance lessons
Friday	sleepover party
Saturday	make Halloween costume
Sunday	go to Amanda's house

1. When does Marcy make a costume? _____

2. What day is the birthday dinner? _____

3. What day is the sleepover party? _____

4. When does Marcy have dance lessons?

_____ _____

_____ , _____

5. What day does she have plans with Amanda? _____

116 **Word Group Four**

Your Week

Fill in the days of the week in order, and write in something you do each day.

Word Box

Wednesday	Saturday
Sunday	Monday
Thursday	Tuesday
Friday	

What is your favorite day of the week?

_____

- -

_____

Day to Day

Read each sentence. Write the day of the week it describes.

Word Box

Sunday	Tuesday	Thursday	Saturday
Monday	Wednesday	Friday	

1. The Norse believed in a god named Woden. This day was once

called Wodnesdaeg. _____

2. Named after Thor, the god of thunder and lightning, this day _____

used to be called Thuresdaeg. _____

3. This day used to be called monan daeg, day of the moon.

_____

_____

4. Once called Tiwesdaeg, this day was named after Tiw, god _____

of war. _____

5. Frigg was a kind and beautiful goddess of nature and love. _____

This day used to be called Frigedaeg. _____

6. During the time of the Roman Empire, this meant "day of _____

the sun." _____

What Day Am I?

Draw a line from the riddles to their answers.

1. Some people think I'm spelled strangely because I have a silent **d**. What day am I?

2. I start with the same beginning sound you hear in **thanks**! What day am I?

3. People sometimes say "T.G.I.F." about me— "Thank goodness it's ___!" What day am I?

4. I'm named after something you see in the sky. What day am I?

5. The first part of my name rhymes with **news**. What day am I?

6. Some think I'm the best day to play. What day am I?

7. I'm the only day that starts with **M**. What day am I?

Monday

Tuesday

Wednesday

Thursday

Friday

Saturday

Sunday

Calendar Fun

Monday	Tuesday	Wednesday	Thursday	Friday	Saturday	Sunday
1	2	3	4	5	6	7
8	9	10	11	12	13	14
15	16	17	18	19	20	21
22	23	24	25	26	27	28
29	30	31				

Look at the calendar. Then circle the answer.

What happens on the first Saturday of the month?

What happens on the second Sunday of the month?

What's special about the second Monday of the month?

What happens on the third Wednesday of the month?

What happens on the first Tuesday of the month?

What happens on the third Friday of the month?

Go! Go! Go!

Word Box

first   second   third   large   cold

Write words from the box to complete the sentences.

_____

The runner wearing blue is coming in _____ .

_____

The runner wearing yellow is in _____ place.

_____

The runner with the red shirt is in _____ place.

_____

The crowd is very _____ .

_____

After the race, they will all need a _____ drink!

Word Math

Can you solve these letter math problems?
Write the picture name, then add and
subtract letters to make a new word.

1.

$— g + c =$

2.

$— b + sm =$

3.

$— sh + k =$

----

4. Saturday $—$ Satur $+$  $=$

Monkey Business

In each set of words, this monkey took away the same letter. Write the missing letter. Write all the missing letters in order on the lines. They spell out the answer to the riddle!

1. _ econd

   _ mall

   Tue _ day

   Thur _ day ____

   The missing letter is ____ .

3. co _ d

   sma _ _

   _ arge ____

   The missing letter is ____ .

2. kee _

   ke _ t ____

   The missing letter is ____ .

4. f _ rst

   Fr _ day

   th _ rd ____

   The missing letter is ____ .

5. firs _

   kep _

   _ hird ____

   The missing letter is ____ .

What did the banana do when the monkey chased it?

___ ___ ___ ___ ___

- - - - - - - - - - - - - - - - -

It ___ ___ ___ ___ ___ !

   1   2   3   4   5

What Kind of Day?

Write each word from the word box in the correct box.

Word Box

cold	Tuesday	Friday	Monday	small
short	long	large	Saturday	Thursday

Adjectives (describing words)

_____

- - - - - - - - - - - -

_____

_____

- - - - - - - - - - - -

_____

_____

- - - - - - - - - - - -

_____

_____

- - - - - - - - - - - -

_____

Days of the week

_____

- - - - - - - - - - - -

_____

_____

- - - - - - - - - - - -

_____

_____

- - - - - - - - - - - -

_____

_____

- - - - - - - - - - - -

_____

Feather in Your Cap

Write the word that rhymes with all the feather words.
Choose from the words in the box.

Word Box

small   keep   third   cold

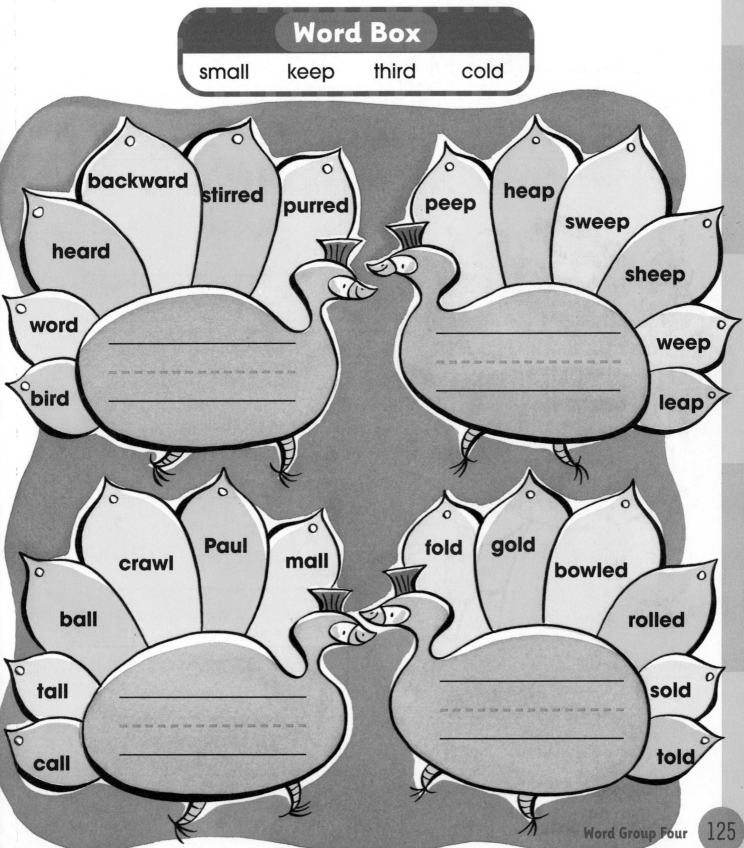

backward   stirred   purred
heard
word
bird

_____
- - - - - - - - - -
_____

peep   heap   sweep
sheep
weep
leap

_____
- - - - - - - - - -
_____

crawl   Paul   mall
ball
tall
call

_____
- - - - - - - - - -
_____

fold   gold   bowled
rolled
sold
told

_____
- - - - - - - - - -
_____

Look Closely!

There are smaller words hiding in each of these words.
Can you find them? Write them on the lines.

Example: b r o t h e r

her   broth   the

small

_____ _____

Friday

_____ _____

Monday _____

_____ _____

Saturday

_____ _____

Six Snails

Look at the picture. Then complete the sentences with the correct word from the box.

Word Box

cold	second	first	large	small	Saturday

_____

The first snail is _____ .

_____

The second snail is _____ .

_____

The third snail is _____ .

_____

The fourth snail looks exactly like the _____ snail.

The fifth snail is happy because he had a long week,

_____

and it is finally _____ !

_____

The sixth snail wishes he was _____ in line!

Scrambled Story

Look at these pictures. Put them in order by writing first, second, and third under each picture.

Draw lines to match the word with another way to say it.

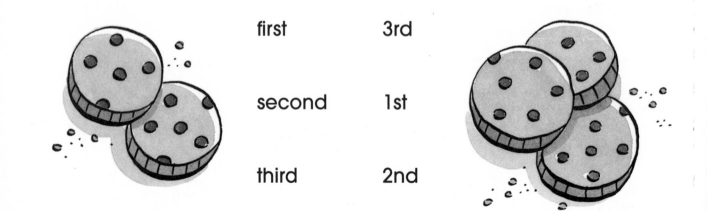

first   3rd

second   1st

third   2nd

Adjective Riddles

Finish the riddles using words from the box.

Word Box

cold   large   small

Itty-bitty, mini-moo,

Teeny-tiny, little too,

Ask me what I'm really like,

And that's what I'll tell you.

_____

- - - - - - - - - - - - - -

What adjective am I? _____

An elephant, the moon.

A dinosaur, a barge.

I am a big adjective,

_____

- - - - - - - - - - - - - -

My name is _____ .

What do I describe?

Ask me and I'll say

Ice cream, ice cubes, icicles,

A chilly winter day.

_____

- - - - - - - - - - - - - -

What adjective am I? _____

What's So Funny?

Draw lines from the jokes to their answers.

third

Moo-nday

Friday

What day can you never

get hard-boiled eggs?

What do you call the youngest

of a family of three robins?

The _____ bird.

What day do cows like to

make all their noises?

Every Picture Tells a Story

Draw a line from each sentence to the picture it describes.

It's cold outside.

The chick is small.

He keeps his hair very short.

An elephant is large.

Alphabet Ladder

Put these words in ABC order on the ladder. Start at the bottom of the ladder and climb all the way to the top!

first

cold

Scientist's Journal

Tyrone visited a butterfly house. Help him finish his science journal. Choose from the words in the box.

Word Box

large	first	cold	Saturday
small	kept	Monday	

_____

On _____ my class visited a butterfly house in the

_____

science museum. It is a _____ room. Plants,

_____

flowers, and butterflies live there! The room is _____

_____

very warm for the butterflies. It can never get _____ .

_____

The _____ thing I saw when I walked in was a

_____

_____ yellow butterfly. It landed on half of an

orange and started eating. I liked the butterfly house. I'm going

_____

back on _____ to see the cocoon display.

I liked it so much I think I'll move in!

First, Second, Third

Finish the sentences using words from the word box.

Word Box

first aid	third
first place	first
first lady	second
secondhand	

1. I joined the _____ _____ pie-eating contest.

I hope I win _____ _____.

2. A gold medal means _____ prize, a silver

means _____, and a bronze means _____.

3. It is helpful to know _____ _____ in case

anyone gets hurt.

4. The president's wife is called the _____ _____.

5. My big sister gives me her clothes when she gets too big for them.

They are _____ clothes.

In the Cold

Finish the sentences using words from the box.

Word Box

cold cuts	cold feet
catch a cold	cold

1. Winter in the north is _____ . _____

2. To have _____ _____ is to get

nervous at the last minute.

3. Meats sliced very thin for sandwiches are

_____ _____

called _____ _____ .

4. Mom always says to wear my hat or I'll

_____ _____

_____ _____ .

What a Day!

How many words can you make from the letters in these three days of the week? Give yourself three minutes to write as many as you can!

Friday

fir

Saturday

Sunday

Snow Day!

Here are pictures from Melissa's snow day. Use the words in the box to finish the sentences.

Word Box

small	Tuesday	keep
first	large	cold

_____, December 5th was the

_____ snow day of the year!

It was so _____ !

I built a _____ snowman

and a _____ snowman.

I built an igloo to _____ warm.

Every Which Way

Complete the arrows with words that fit.
Choose from the words in the box.

Word Box

second   Saturday   Tuesday   small   third   Thursday

Word Stairs

Help Liza get down the stairs.
Write the words that fit on each step.

Word Box

small large second third kept

eggs

dot

dark

Short For?

Each day of the week has its own abbreviation.
Draw lines to connect the abbreviations
to the matching words.

Mon.	Tuesday
Tues.	Wednesday
Wed.	Saturday
Thurs.	Sunday
Fri.	Monday
Sat.	Thursday
Sun.	Friday

Mon.

day

Sight Word Spelling Bee Board Game

You'll Need:

- the game board on pages 142–143
- a number cube or die
- a game piece for each player (a coin or a bean will work)
- pencil and paper

How to Play

Roll the number cube or die. Move your piece the number of dots in the cube.

If you land on a hive, read the sentence and then write the answer on your paper. Have another player check your answer. If you land on a **honey drop**, read the word out loud, then look away and write it on your paper. Check your answer by matching it to the word in the honey drop. If your answer is correct, stay where you are. If your answer is incorrect, go back to where you were and try spelling again on your next turn.

The first person to reach **FINISH** wins!

Help the bee get to the flowers!

Start

Sunday

Spell the word that means the opposite of short.

Spell the day of the week that comes after Sunday.

Spell the word that means big and starts with l.

cold

small

Monday

Spell the day of the week that comes after Wednesday.

Spell the word that is the opposite of "gave away."

third

first

Thursday

113 1. Monday, Tuesday; 2. Wednesday; 3. Thursday; 4. Friday; 5. Saturday, Sunday

114 cold; First; Second; Third; kept; small, large; keep

115 1. large; 2. small; 3. large; 4. large; 5. small; 6. small

116 1. Saturday; 2. Monday; 3. Friday; 4. Tuesday, Thursday; 5. Sunday

117 answers will vary

118 1. Wednesday; 2. Thursday; 3. Monday; 4. Tuesday; 5. Friday; 6. Sunday

119 1. Wednesday; 2. Thursday; 3. Friday; 4. Sunday; 5. Tuesday; 6. Saturday; 7. Monday

120 circle: pizza party; piano recital; no school symbol; birthday cake; soccer ball; pillow

121 first; second; third; large; cold

122 cold; small; keep; Sunday

123 1. s; 2. p; 3. l; 4. i; 5. t; split

124 **Adjectives:** cold, short, long, large, small;
Days of the week: Monday, Tuesday, Saturday, Friday, Thursday

125 third; keep; small; cold

126 choose among: am, as, Sam, all, mall; rid; day; on; day; sat; at; day

127 large; small; cold; second; Saturday; first

128 second; first; third; first/1st; second/2nd; third/3rd

129 small; large; cold

130 Friday; third; Moo-nday

131 draw lines to match photos to text

132 cold; first; Friday; kept; large, Monday; small; Sunday; third; Tuesday

133 Monday; large; kept; cold; first; small; Saturday

134 1. first place; 2. first, second, third; 3. first aid; 4. first lady; 5. secondhand

135 1. cold; 2. cold feet; 3. cold cuts; 4. catch a cold

136 answers will vary

137 Tuesday, first; cold; large; small; keep

138 see right

139 see right

140 Mon./Monday; Tues./Tuesday;
Wed./Wednesday; Thurs./Thursday;
Fri./Friday; Sat./Saturday; Sun./Sunday

page 139

page 138

On Friday, Ling remembered the bunch of small bananas. She ran home from school. She ran into the kitchen. Sam ran after her. Ling opened the freezer door. There they were: the bananas!

And they turned out to be a tasty treat!

8

fold & assemble

Scholastic 100 Words Kids Need to Read by 2nd Grade, Word Group 4

1

Who Hid the Bananas?

Written by Anne Schreiber

Illustrated by Greg Paprocki

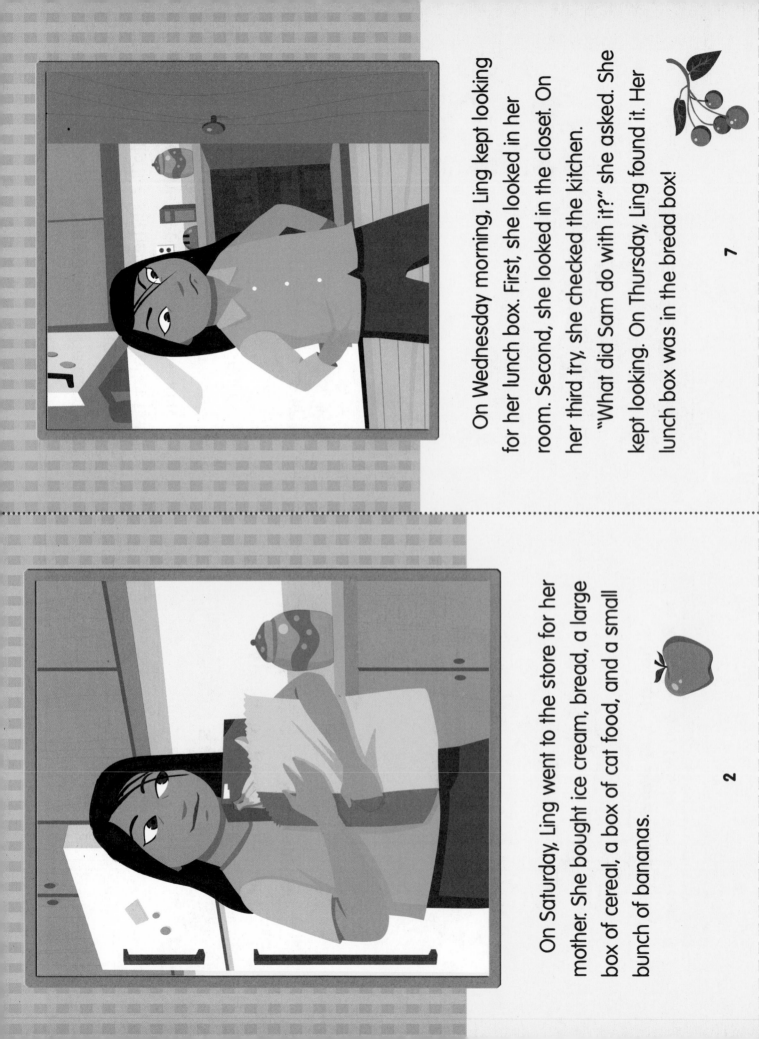

On Wednesday morning, Ling kept looking for her lunch box. First, she looked in her room. Second, she looked in the closet. On her third try, she checked the kitchen.

"What did Sam do with it?" she asked. She kept looking. On Thursday, Ling found it. Her lunch box was in the bread box!

On Saturday, Ling went to the store for her mother. She bought ice cream, bread, a large box of cereal, a box of cat food, and a small bunch of bananas.

On Tuesday, the cat meowed and meowed. Ling grabbed a box from the top shelf. She filled the cat's bowl. The cat kept meowing. Ling looked down.

"That's not cat food!" she said. She looked at the box. It was the cereal. "That Sam!" she said. She checked the low shelf. There was the cat food. Luckily, no one had tried to eat it for breakfast!

Ling's little brother Sam wanted to put the food away. Ling told him where everything was kept.

"First, put the ice cream in the freezer to keep it cold," she said. "The bread goes in the bread box to stay fresh. Put the bananas on the table. Put the cereal on the low shelf. Then you can reach it. Put the cat food on the high shelf. Then the cat can't reach it."

On Sunday, Ling went to the freezer to get some ice cream. She looked a first time. She looked around a second time. She looked a third time. Then she found it on the table.

"This is not ice cream anymore," Ling said. "It's not even cold cream. What a mess!"

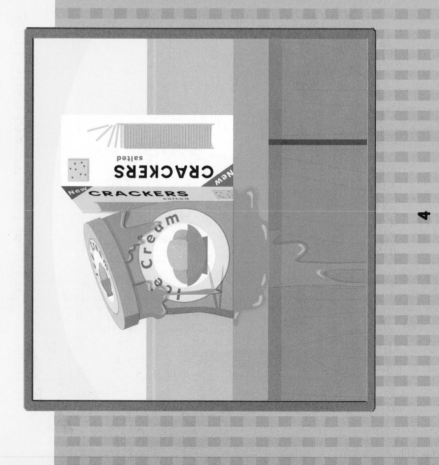

On Monday, Ling looked in her backpack for her lunch box. She found a large bag. It was the bread. Sam had left it in her backpack. Ling had bread for lunch — lots of it!

Word Search

Find all the words from the box in the word search.

```
b  t  h  s  c  h  e  w  g
a  u  s  j  m  v  v  o  h
s  n  i  s  a  b  e  s  t
f  u  y  d  a  k  r  e  r
e  w  o  m  a  n  y  n  t
w  m  t  s  e  l  g  v  h
x  i  t  h  e  m  d  u  e
o  s  i  n  e  e  q  t  i
q  i  m  s  d  y  z  a  r
```

Hello!

Fill in the blanks with the right words from the word box.

Word Box

better	thank	town	hello
please	help	good-bye	

_____

- - - - - - - - - - - - - -

1. Can you _____ me with my

   homework?   _____

                                 - - - - - - - - - - - -

2. I was sick yesterday. Now I feel _____.

                          _____

                          - - - - - - - - - - - -

3. Two very polite words are _____

   _____

   - - - - - - - - - - -

   and _____ you!

                          _____

                          - - - - - - - - - - - -

4. Do you live in a city or a _____?

                    _____

                    - - - - - - - - - -

5. In the morning I say _____ to my

   friends at school.   _____

                          - - - - - - - - - -

   At the end of the day I say _____.

Our Town

Fnish the sentences using these words: **best**, **better**, **every**, **many**, **please**, **town**. Hint: You may have to use some words more than once or a capital letter.

_____

Our _____ is a great place to spend the weekend.

_____

There are _____ things to do for fun. We have the

_____

_____ apples in the country and a beautiful lake.

_____

_____ people have houses at the lake in our

_____   _____

_____ . They come here _____ weekend.

_____

The ice cream store in town is _____ than

_____

others I've tried. _____ come and visit.

See you soon!

Words & Pictures

Draw a line from each sentence to the picture it describes.

This is their dog.

She has many crayons.

He is waving to say hello.

She raises her hand to ask for help.

He blew a few bubbles.

Me, Me, Me, Me!

Tell about yourself. Check **yes** or **no** after each sentence.

	Yes	No
I live in a town, not a city.	☐	☐
I have many freckles.	☐	☐
I take a bus to school every day of the school week.	☐	☐
I think strawberry ice cream is better than chocolate.	☐	☐
I like a few different sports.	☐	☐

Now draw a picture of yourself in your town or city.

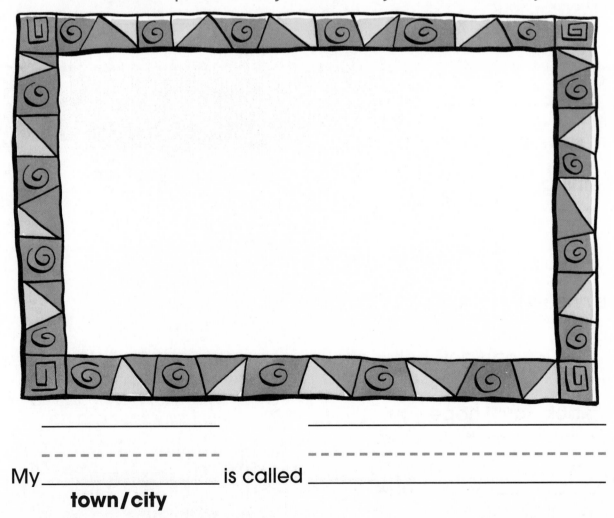

My _____ is called _____ .
town/city

Monster Manners

Monster rules are the opposite of our rules. Use words from the word box to finish the rules charts.

People Rules

_____

- - - - - - - - - - - - - -

Brush your teeth _____

day.

_____

- - - - - - - - - - - - - -

Say _____ when

you want something.

_____

- - - - - - - - - - - - - -

Say _____ you

when someone gives you

something.

_____

- - - - - - - - - - - - - -

_____ your friends

if they need it.

When your friend gets better after

being sick, say "I hope you

_____

- - - - - - - - - - - - - -

feel _____ now."

Word Box

better	good-bye	help	thank
every	hello	please	

_____

- - - - - - - - - - - - - -

Say _____ when

you meet someone, and

_____

- - - - - - - - - - - - - -

_____ when you

leave.

Monster Rules

Never brush your teeth!

_____

- - - - - - - - - - - - - -

Never say _____ or

_____

- - - - - - - - - - - - - -

_____ you.

Don't greet people you meet or

say anything when you leave.

_____

- - - - - - - - - - - - - -

Don't say _____

_____

- - - - - - - - - - - - - -

or _____ .

Hide-and-Seek Words

There are smaller words hiding in each of these words.
Can you find them? Write them on the lines.

Example: (b e) a u t (i f) u l

---be---   ---if---

be   if

every _____ _____

_____ _____

them _____ _____ _____

_____ _____ _____

many _____ _____ _____

_____ _____ _____

town _____ _____

_____ _____

Word Math

Can you solve these letter math problems?
Write the picture name, then add and subtract
letters to make a new word.

— cl + t = _____

_____

— n + b = _____

_____

+ y = _____

_____

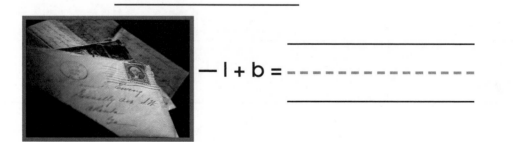

— b + th = _____

_____

— l + b = _____

_____

The Missing Letters

This shark ate the same letter in each set of words.
Write the missing letter at the end of each set.

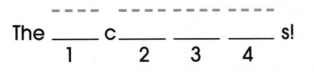

1. be __ t   ____
   plea __ e   - - - -
   The missing letter is ____.

2. __ ny
   m __ ny
   ple __ se   ____
   th __ nk   - - - -
   The missing letter is ____.

3. p __ ease
   he __ p   ____
   he __ __ o   - - - -
   The missing letter is ____.

4. __ v __ ry
   f __ w
   th __ ir
   th __ m
   b __ st
   b __ tter
   pl __ as __
   h __ lp
   good-by __   ____
   h __ llo   - - - -
   The missing letter is ——.

Now write all the missing letters in order on the lines.
They spell out the answer to this riddle!

What part of a fish weighs the most?

____ ____ ____ ____

- - - -   - - - - - - - - - - - - - -

The ____ c ____ ____ s!
    1   2   3   4

Heads . . . Down!

Finish the sentences with words from the word box.

_____

There is a _____ called Upside-Down! Everything there

is upside-down. The sidewalks there are very clean because people

_____

walk around on _____ hands. The people in

_____

Upside-Down like it _____ than living right-side up. They

_____

all think it's the _____ ! Other people think that instead of

being Upside-Down town, it should be renamed Backwards Town,

_____

because when people see each other they say " _____ "

_____

and when they leave they say " _____ ."

Stacking Up!

Choose words from the box that will fill the spaces. Then answer the riddle by writing the boxed letters in the red boxes on the line.

Word Box

every	help	better	town	any
please	many	thank	hello	

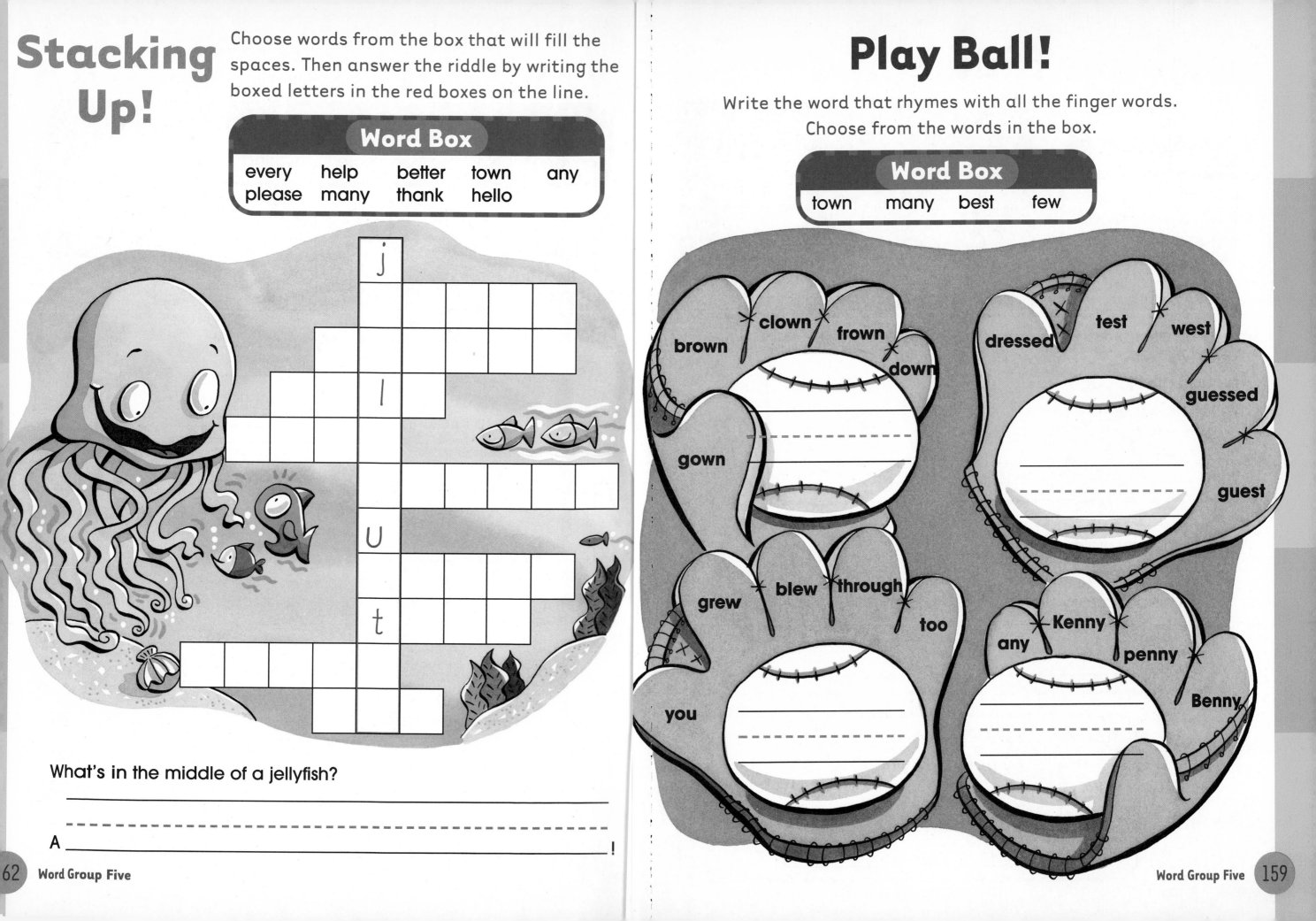

j

l

u

t

What's in the middle of a jellyfish?

A _____!

Play Ball!

Write the word that rhymes with all the finger words. Choose from the words in the box.

Word Box

town	many	best	few

brown clown frown down
gown

dressed test west
guessed
guest

grew blew through
too
you

any Kenny
penny
Benny

Finish the Riddle

Finish the riddles with words from the word box.

Word Box

thank	few
hello	please
good-bye	many

We're total opposites,
Through and through.
We tell how much.

_____   _____

We're _____ and _____ .

Some say we're magic.
Mom agrees.
It's helpful to say us.

_____   _____

We're _____ you and _____ .

You can usually find us at a beginning or end.
It's nice to say us to family and friends.
Who are we?

_____   _____

_____ and _____ .

Many Anys

Finish the sentences using the correct word from the word box.

Word Box

anyone   anywhere   anymore   anything   anyway   anytime

_____

1. I don't sleep in a crib _____ .

2. The bus is full. I can't find _____ to sit down.

3. Does _____ know the answer?

4. "Have some," she said.

   _____

   "I can't eat it all, _____ ."

5. This store is always open.

   You can shop here _____ .

6. Did you bring _____ sweet for snack today?

Pairing Off

Fill the boxes with words that fit. Choose from the words in the box. Hint: Each puzzle contains two words that are a pair.

Word Box

good-bye   please   few   hello   every   thank

The Bake Sale

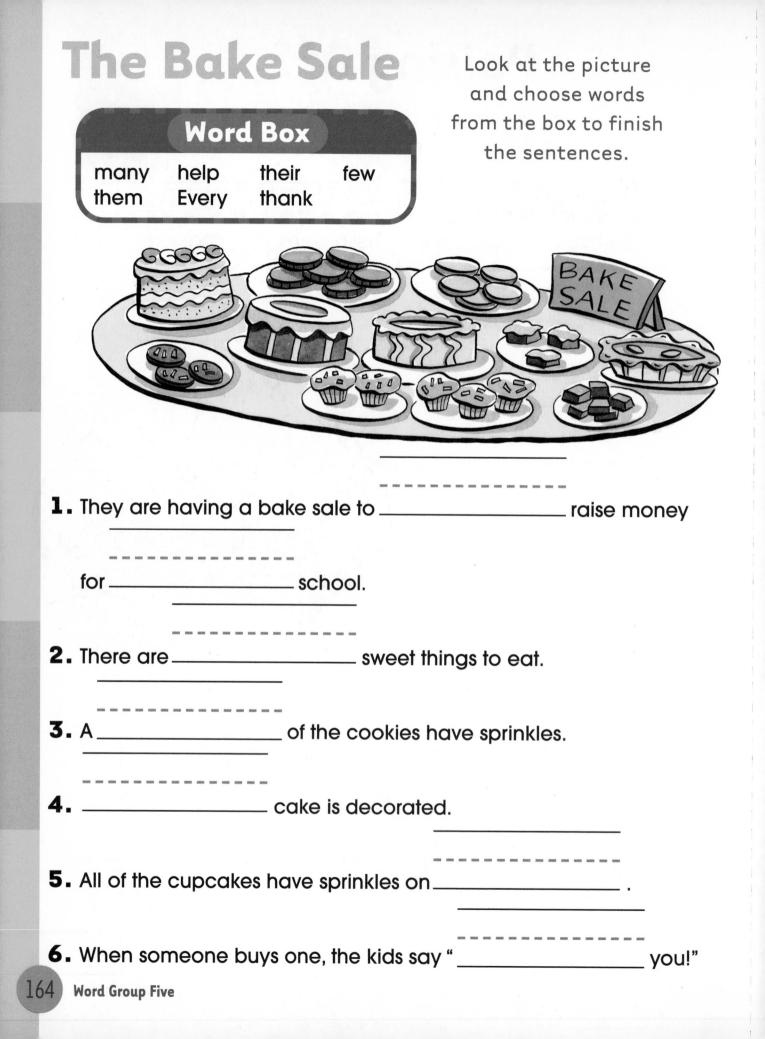

Look at the picture and choose words from the box to finish the sentences.

Word Box

many	help	their	few
them	Every	thank	

1. They are having a bake sale to _____ raise money

for _____ school.

2. There are _____ sweet things to eat.

3. A _____ of the cookies have sprinkles.

4. _____ cake is decorated.

5. All of the cupcakes have sprinkles on_____ .

6. When someone buys one, the kids say " _____ you!"

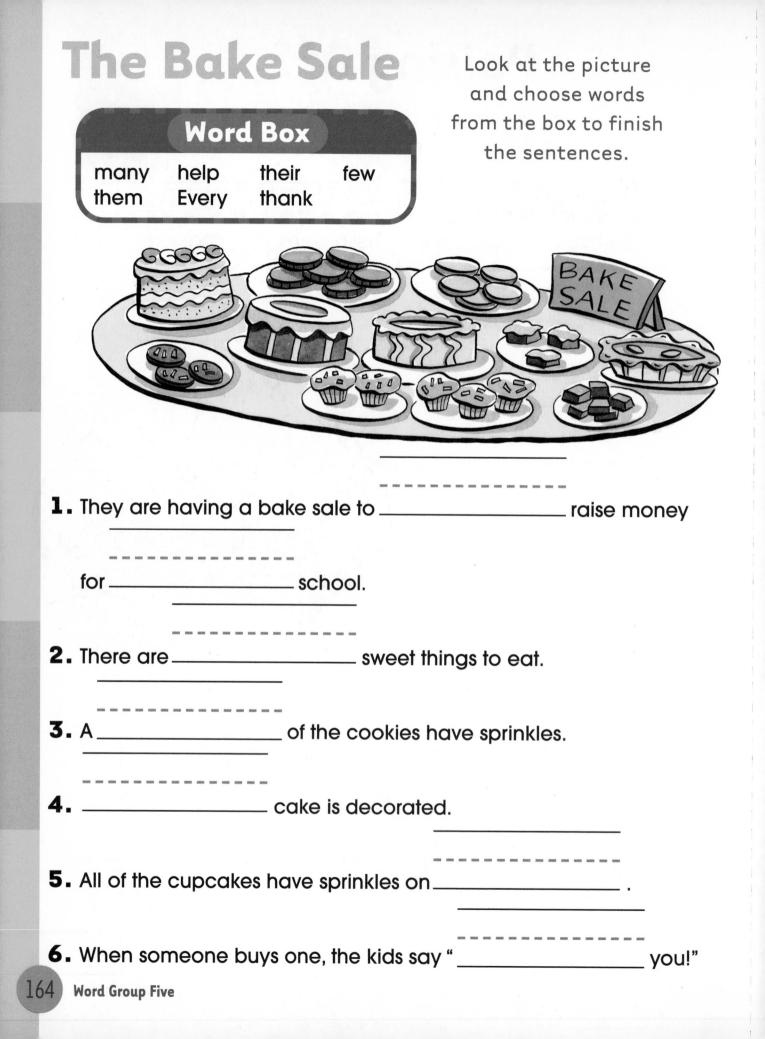

Betty the Baker

Choose words from the box to finish the tongue twister. Then say it five times out loud!
Hint: Use a capital letter.

Word Box

better
please
any
help

Betty made a batch of bitter batter.

_____ _____

"_____ _____ me

_____

make my batter _____!"

"I can make this batter_____.

_____

Butter makes _____

_____

batter _____!"

The Field Trip

Sally's class went on a field trip to the aquarium. Look at the pictures. Then use the words in the box to finish the sentences. Hint: You may need to use a capital letter.

_____ kid in the

class came on the trip. There

were so _____ of us

that the bus was full.

At the aquarium we saw a

_____ starfish in a tank.

We saw seals playing.

They balanced balls on

_____ noses!

We had a great day. I liked it

_____ than the zoo.

It was the _____ field

trip we've had this year.

Puzzle Pieces

Draw lines to match the first syllables
to the second syllables.

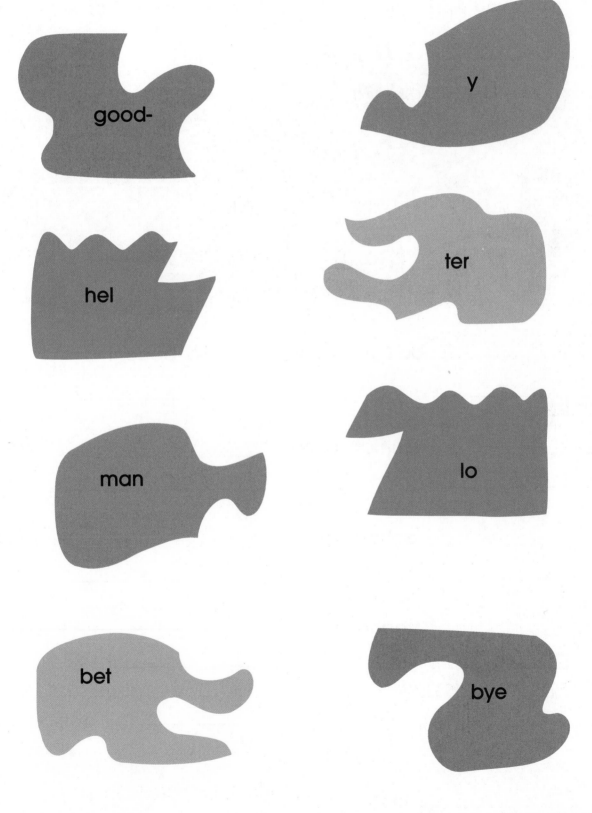

good-

y

hel

ter

man

lo

bet

bye

The Last Day of School

Good-bye, school! Hello, summer!
It's the last day of school! Write **Hello** or **Good-bye** on each line to tell what you would say to each of these things when school ends.

Good-bye, homework! Hello, beach!

_____
_____ , suntan lotion!

_____
_____ , school bus!

_____
_____ , teacher!

_____
_____ , swimming!

_____
_____ , school!

_____
_____ , summer fun!

_____
_____ , fireflies!

_____
_____ , getting up early!

A-Maze-ing!

Follow the path of words with the short **e** sound, as in egg.

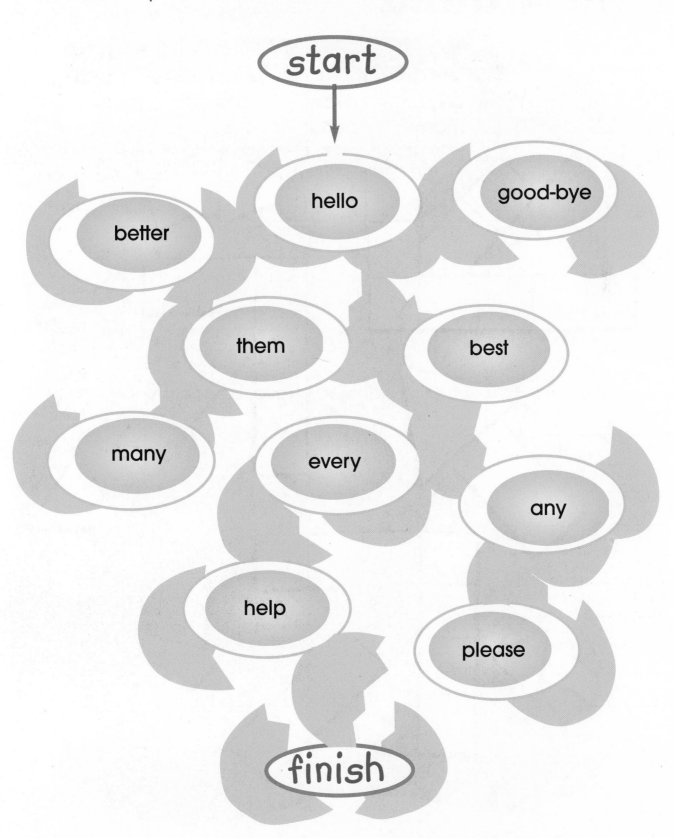

start

hello

good-bye

better

them

best

many

every

any

help

please

finish

Up, Down, and All Around

Write the words that fit in the arrows. Choose from the words in the box.

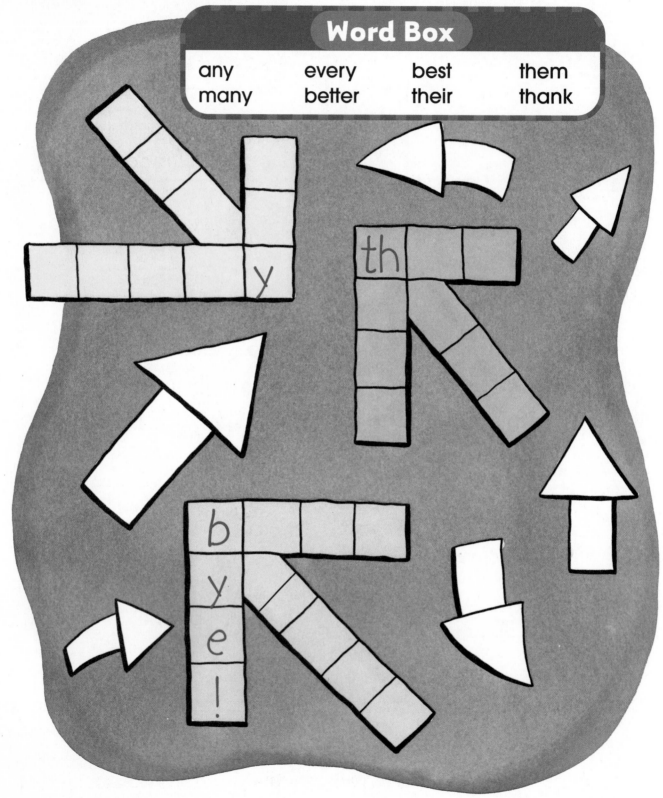

Word Box

any	every	best	them
many	better	their	thank

Color the arrow that points to a short word for **good-bye**.

A Word Bouquet

Use words from the box to answer the questions.

Word Box

hello   few   any   many   best   thank

1. Which 3-letter word rhymes with **drew**? _____

2. Which 4-letter word means **a lot**? _____

3. Which 5-letter word is another word for **hi**?_____

4. Which 5-letter word starts with **th** and is usually followed by the _____

   word **you**? _____

5. Which 4-letter word rhymes with **vest**? _____

6. Which 3-letter word ends like **every** and **many**? _____

The Magic Words

How many words can you make from the letters in these two "magic words"?

please

_____

- - - - - - - - - - - - - - -

_____

- - - - - - - - - - - - - - -

_____

- - - - - - - - - - - - - - -

_____

- - - - - - - - - - - - - - -

_____

- - - - - - - - - - - - - - -

thank

_____

- - - - - - - - - - - - - - -

_____

- - - - - - - - - - - - - - -

_____

- - - - - - - - - - - - - - -

_____

- - - - - - - - - - - - - - -

_____

- - - - - - - - - - - - - - -

Better . . . Best!

Word Box

good   better   best

chocolate	vanilla	strawberry
better	*good*	*best*

soccer	jump rope	baseball

walking to school	taking the bus	riding my bike

getting up early	sleeping late	going to bed late

hamburger	hot dog	french fries

Going Down

Help the explorer come down the the mountain. Write the words that fit in each step of the way.

Word Box

best   every   good-bye
please town

n a p

y
o
u
n
g

What's So Funny?

Finish the riddles. Choose from the words in the box.

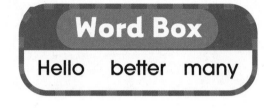

Word Box

Hello   better   many

How does one man turn into a crowd?

_____

- - - - - - - - - - - - - - -

When you add a y and he becomes _____ .

How do you make the best cake?

_____

- - - - - - - - - - - - - - -

Use a _____ batter.

What did the whipped cream say when it jumped on the wobbly green stuff?

_____

- - - - - - - - - - - -

_____ , Jello!

Alphabet Beanstalk

Help Jack get up the beanstalk!
Write these words in alphabetical order.
Start at the bottom of the beanstalk
and climb all the way to the clouds!

Word Box

every	please
many	help
few	town

Underwater Words

Write the word from the box that means the same as the word on each octopus leg.

Word Box

large
small
cold

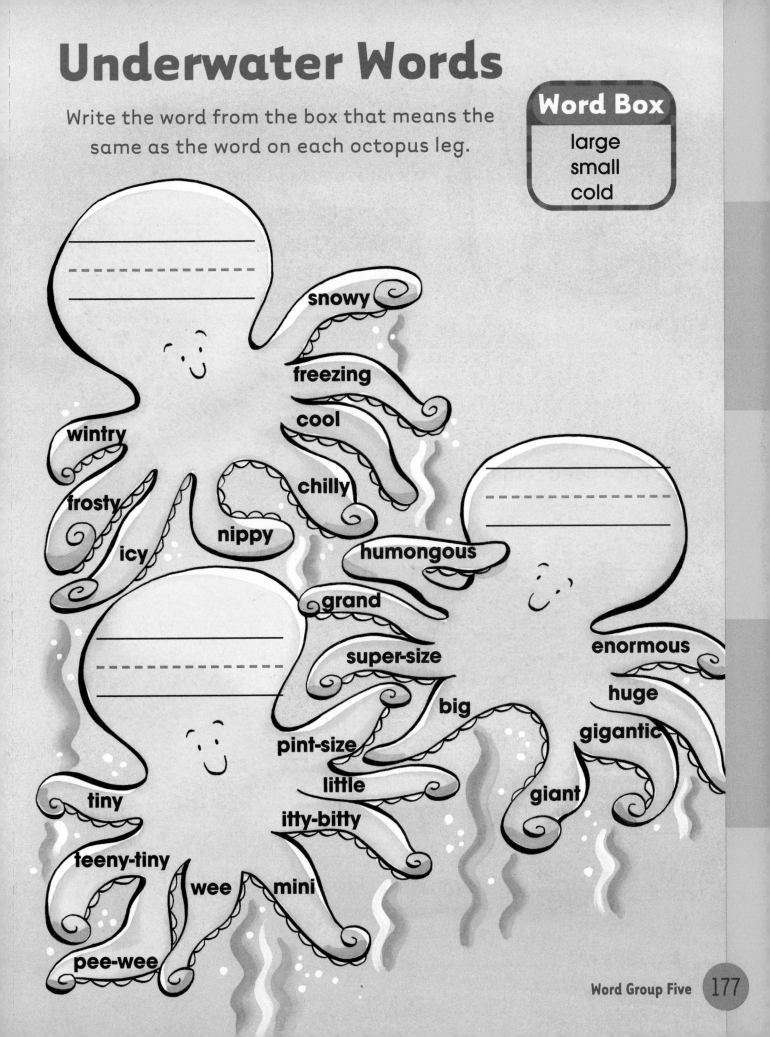

snowy

freezing

cool

chilly

nippy

wintry

frosty

icy

humongous

grand

super-size

big

pint-size

little

itty-bitty

enormous

huge

gigantic

giant

tiny

teeny-tiny

wee

mini

pee-wee

Silly Soup

Use words from the box to finish this recipe for a very silly soup. (Hint: Don't try making this soup at home! Yech!)

Word Box

help	thank	every	best
them	please	better	few

Silly Soup

_____

If you have a sweet tooth, here's the _____ recipe for

soup! You'll need some _____ from your friends!

Remember to ask _____ nicely and say _____ .

Take _____ thing sweet you have in the kitchen, like sugar,

jelly, and honey. Put them in the pot and heat it up! Add chocolate

chips and chocolate milk.

What would make the soup taste even _____? Sprinkle

a _____ jellybeans on top before serving!

Your guests will _____ you!

Buggy Town

Read this poem out loud. Can you find all these words:
any, best, better, every, few, good-bye, hello, help,
many, please, thank, their, them, town? Underline them.

Deep in the yard, on a green patch of ground,

Lies a hidden place called Buggy Town.

Many insects live here, not just a few.

Please watch where you walk,

they'll get under your shoe.

In their grassy town, all the bugs come and go.

You can hear them call out "Good-bye!" or "Hello!"

Every bug mind its manners and says "thank you" or "please."

(Except, of course, for those rude bugs, the fleas!)

The bugs help each other and no one is a pest.

For any and all bugs, Buggy Town is better than best!

Word Group 5 Answer Key

149 see right

150 1. help; 2. better; 3. please, thank;
4. town; 5. hello, good-bye

151 town; many; best; Many, town; every;
better; Please

152 match text to photos

153 answers will vary

154 **People Rules:** every; please; thank;
Help; better; hello; good-bye
Monster Rules: please; thank; hello; good-bye

155 choose among: ever, very; he, hem, the; man, an, any;
to, own, tow

156 town; best; many; thank; better

157 1. s; 2. a; 3. l; 4. e; scales

158 town; their; better; best; good-bye, hello

159 town; best; few; many

160 many, few; thank, please; hello, good-bye

161 1. anymore; 2. anywhere; 3. anyone;
4. anyway; 5. anytime; anything

162 see right; jellybutton

163 see right

164 1. help, their; 2. many; 3. few; 4. Every;
5. them; 6. thank

165 Please, help; better; better; any, better

166 Every, many; few, their; better; best

167 bet/ter; man/y; hel/lo; good/bye

168 Hello; Good-bye; Good-bye; Hello;
Good-bye; Hello; Hello; Good-bye

169 see right

170 see right

171 1. few; 2. many; 3. hello; 4. thank; 5. best; 6. any

172 answers will vary

173 answers will vary

174 see right

175 many; better; hello

176 every; few; help; many; please; town

177 cold; small; large

178 best; help; them, please; every; better, few, thank

179 underline: Many, few; Please their; town; them;
Good-bye, Hello; Every, thank, please; help;
any, better, best

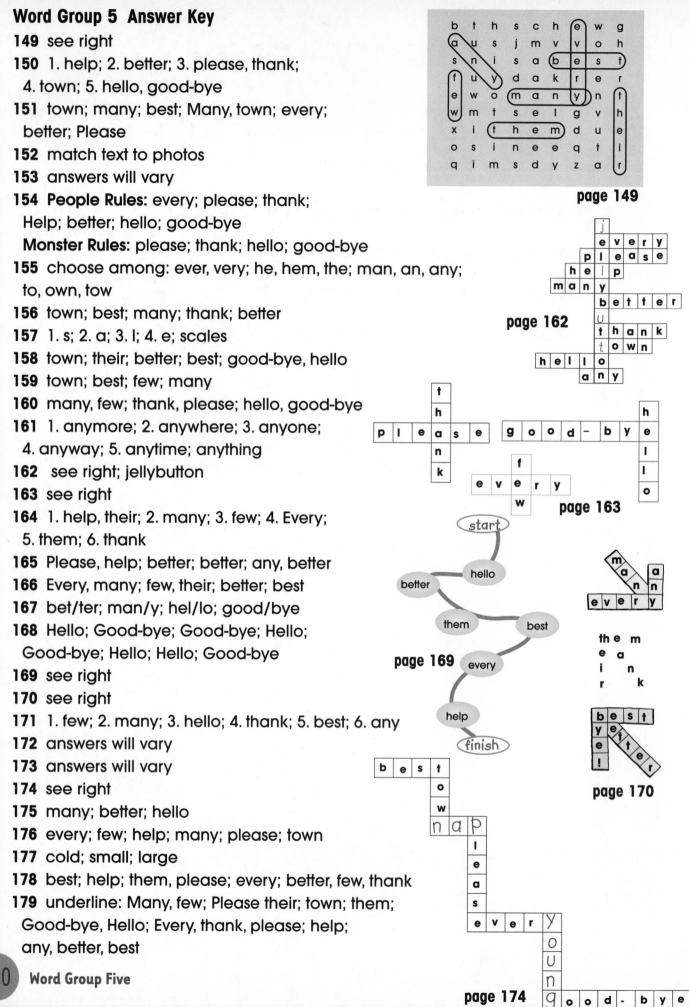

page 149

page 162

page 163

page 169

page 170

page 174

8

"Mo and Jo," said the banker. "You make the best pies in town."

"No," said Mo. She smiled at Flo.

"Today Flo made the best pies."

The banker bought another of Flo's pies before he left.

"Good-bye!" said Mo and Jo and Flo.

Then they all had some pie!

fold & assemble

1

The Best Pies in Town

Written by Kathryn McKeon

Illustrated Valeria Petrone

Scholastic 100 Words Kids Need to Read by 2nd Grade, Word Group 5

Mo and Jo gave Flo many tips on how to make any pie better.

Flo made a few cherry pies. She made a few apple pies.

The banker came into the shop. He ate every bite of one of Flo's new pies.

7

Mo and Jo made the best pies in town.

"Their cherry pie is better than the best slice," said the pizza man.

"Their apple pie is better than the best cone," said the ice cream man.

"Few pies are better," said the banker.

2

Flo took a bite of one of her pies.

"Yuck!" she said.

"Every pie I make needs help. Can you help me make a better pie?"

"We can help," Mo and Jo told their sister.

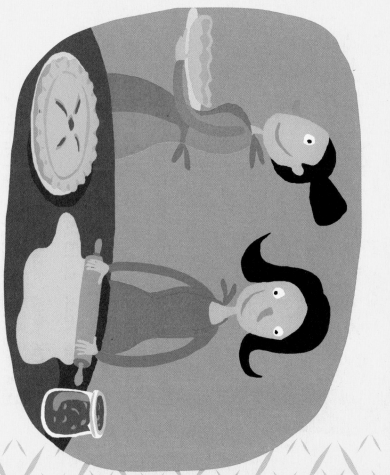

Every day, Mo and Jo made many pies.

Their pie shop was always busy.

Then one day, Mo and Jo's sister Flo came to town.

"Hello, Mo. Hello, Jo," said Flo.

"Hello, Flo," said Mo and Jo.

"Oh, my," said Mo.

"Oh, dear," said Jo.

They made many funny faces.

"You don't like them?" said Flo.

"They are not the best," said Mo.

"I have had better," said Jo.

Flo gave Mo and Jo two pies. "Please try them," she said. "I just made them this morning."

"Thank you," said Mo.

"Thank you," said Jo.

They each took a few bites of Flo's pies.

Word Search

Finish the sentences with words from the box.

Word Box

after	now
Before	open
here	Soon
how	

_____
- - - - - - - - - - - - - -

1. Hello, _____are you?

_____
- - - - - - - - - - - - - - -

2. The show is starting right _____!

_____
- - - - - - - - - - - - - - -

3. The opposite of closed is _____.

_____
- - - - - - - - - - - - - -

4. I said to my dog, "Come _____ , boy!"

_____
- - - - - - - - - - - - - -

5. It's almost noon. _____ it will be time for lunch.

_____   _____
- - - - - - - - - - - - -   - - - - - - - - - - - - - -

6. _____ is the opposite of _____.

Where's That Word?

Fill in the blanks with the right words from the box.

Word Box

then   there   what   When   where   why

1. A map tells you _____ things are.

2. A clock tells you _____ time it is.

3. _____ does the bus leave?

4. I wonder _____ the sky is blue.

5. In the morning, I get dressed, _____ I eat breakfast.

6. Look over _____ ! It's a rainbow!

Now, use two of the words from the box in your own sentence.

_____

_____

Extra! Extra!

Read the newspaper article. Then draw lines to connect the answers to their questions.

Children Find Pot of Gold!

Several children found a pot of gold yesterday in a faraway field! "We followed the rainbow to see if there really was a pot of gold at the end," they said. "We just kept walking until we got to the end of the rainbow!"

QUESTIONS

Who found the gold?

What did they find?

When did this happen?

Where did they find the gold?

Why did they follow the rainbow?

How did they find the gold?

ANSWERS

in a faraway field

to see if there was gold at the end

several children

they followed the rainbow

a pot of gold

yesterday

Be a Reporter

Now it is your turn to play reporter. Look at the picture and pretend you are going to write an article about it. What questions will you need to ask? Fill in the blanks to complete each question. Choose from the words in the box.

Word Box

When   Where   What   Why

Bubble Gum Blowing Contest

A

_____
_____ was the goal of the contest?

_____
_____ did the contest happen?

_____
_____ did the contest take place?

_____
_____ did these kids want to be in the contest?

Fairy Fun

Look at this schedule from the Tooth Fairy's date book.
Circle **before** or **after** to tell what happens when.

1. The Tooth Fairy gathers the quarters (before, after) breakfast.

2. She sleeps (before, after) she polishes her wand.

3. She polishes her wand (before, after) her dentist appointment.

4. She takes Leo's tooth (before, after) she takes Samantha's tooth.

5. She takes Justin's tooth (before, after) she takes Sue's tooth.

4 W's

Write the correct words on the lines.
Then complete the crossword puzzle.

Down

_____

- - - - - - - - - - - - - -

1. A map will show you _____ to go.

_____

- - - - - - - - - - - - -

2. A clock tells you _____ time it is.

Across   _____

- - - - - - - - - - - - - -

1. I wonder _____ soap floats.

_____

- - - - - - - - - - - - -

2. _____ the dog chased the cat, the cat ran

under the car.

Here & There

Here's what Mark says about his treehouse.
Fill in the blanks with the words **here** and
there to complete the sentences.

_____

I love it _____ in my treehouse.

_____

I have games and books in _____

_____

Down over _____ , in my real

house, things are different. My family lives

_____

_____ , but I'm the only one

_____

that comes in _____ . My

_____

cat is allowed in both places: _____

_____

AND _____ !

Words Within Words

There are smaller words hiding in each of these words.
Can you find them? Write them on the lines.

Example: (b e) a u t (i f) u l

--- be --- --- if ---

soon
_____ _____
_____ _____

here
_____ _____
_____ _____

where
_____ _____ _____
_____ _____ _____

before
_____ _____
_____ _____

then
_____ _____
_____ _____

there
_____ _____ _____
_____ _____ _____

Letter Math

Can you solve these letter math problems? Write the picture name, then add and subtract letters to make a new word.

_____
— c + h = _ _ _ _ _ _ _ _ _ _ _ _ _ _
_____

_____
- - - - - - - - - -
w + 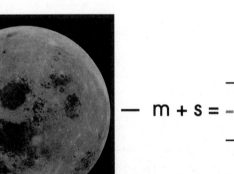 = _ _ _ _ _ _ _ _ _ _ _ _
_____
- - - - - - - - - -
_____

t + = _ _ _ _ _ _ _ _ _ _ _ _ _
_____
- - - - - - - - - -
_____

_____
— m + s = _ _ _ _ _ _ _ _ _ _ _ _ _ _
_____
- - - - - - - - - -

Mystery Letter

In each set of words, the same letter is missing. Write the mystery letter at the end of each set.

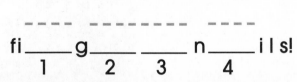

1. _ ow
   soo _
   whe _   _ _ _ _
   The mystery letter is _____ .

2. aft _ r
   b _ for _
   h _ r _
   th _ n
   th _ r _
   wh _ n   _____
   wh _ r _   - - - -
   The mystery letter is _____ .

3. afte _
   befo _ e
   he _ e
   the _ e   _____
   whe _ e   - - - -
   The mystery letter is _____ .

4. _ fter   _____
   wh _ t   - - - -
   The mystery letter is _____ .

Now write all the mystery letters in order on the lines. They spell out the answer to this riddle!

What nails do carpenters hate to hit?

____ _____ ____
- - - - - - - - - - - - -
fi ___ g ___ ___ n ___ i l s!
    1   2   3   4

Up, Up, and Away!

Write each of these words: **why**, **how**, **now**, **when**, **where**, **soon**, **then**, **after**, **before**, **who**, **what**, in the correct hot air balloon.

Question words

Words that tell "when"

Warm Up with Words

Read the words on the squares out loud. In the center of each quilt, write the word that rhymes with all the square words. Choose from the words in the box.

Word Box

here   who   why   then

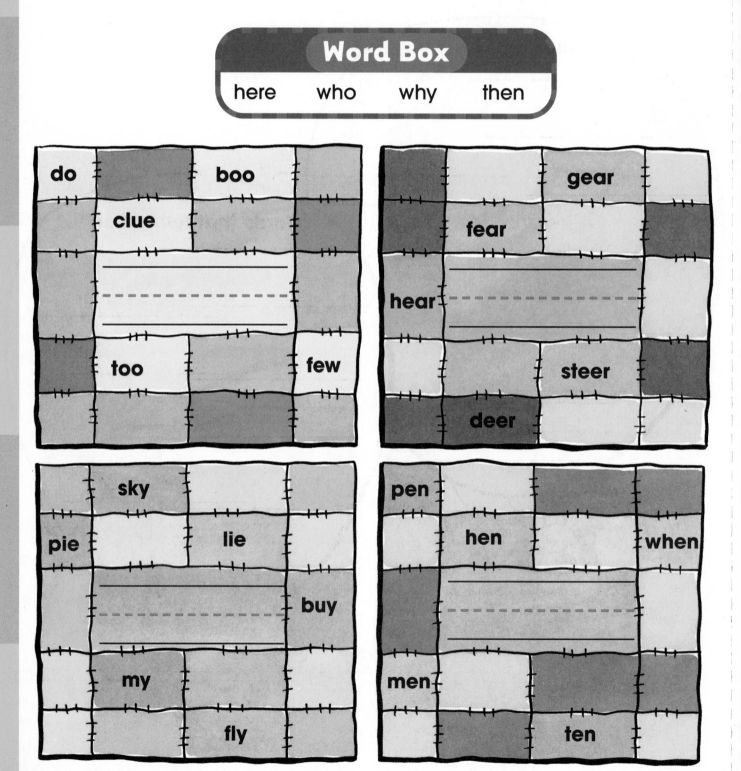

do   boo
clue

too   few

gear
fear
hear

steer
deer

sky
pie   lie
buy
my
fly

pen
hen   when
men
ten

What's So Funny?

Use the words from the box to finish the riddles.

Word Box

How   When   What   Why

_____
- - - - - - - - -
_____ did the chicken cross the playground?

To get to the other slide!

_____
- - - - - - - - -
_____ does the clock strikes thirteen?

When it's time to buy a new clock!

_____
- - - - - - - - -
_____ do you call a nasty pea?

A mean bean!

_____
- - - - - - - - -
_____ do you give a porcupine a bath?

Very carefully!

Open Sesame!

Finish each sentence with a word from the word box.

Word Box

opened	open house
opening	out in the open
open	

_____

1. I _____ the jar of jelly.

2. My dad met my teacher

   _____

   at my school's _____ .

3. You should talk about what makes you mad. You should

   _____ _____ _____ _____

   get it _____ _____ _____ _____ .

   _____

4. The _____ of the new art show is next week.

   _____

5. The sign on the door said "_____ ".

Pile It Up!

Write the words from the box in the spaces where they fit. Hint: One of the words is used twice. Then answer the riddle by writing the letters in the red box on the line.

m
m
w
l
d

What do mermaids have on toast?

- - - - - - - - - - - - - - - -

Pairing Off

Fill the boxes with words that fit.
Choose from the words in the box.
Hint: Each puzzle contains
two words that are a pair.

Word Box

| before | soon | after |
| here | there | now |

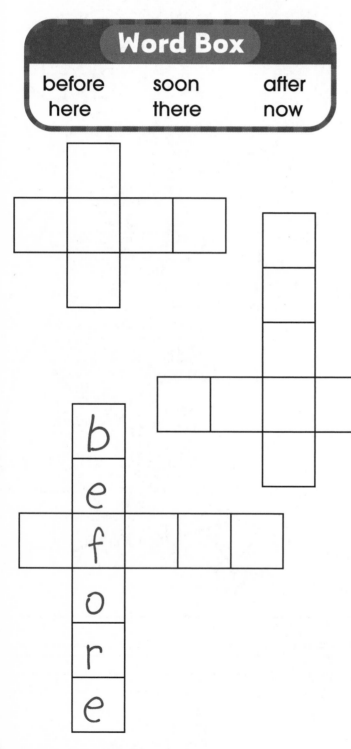

What's Going On?

Draw a line from each sentence to the picture that matches it.

The door is open.

The boy said, "Hello, how are you?"

We live here together.

After dinner, the girl had dessert.

Two's Company

In each group, there is a word that does not belong.
It may have a different spelling pattern.
It might be a different type of word than the others.
Or, it might not rhyme with the others.
Circle the word in each group that does not belong.

after	dog	before

open	how	now

who	what	soon

why	then	there

when	how	where

The Train Trip

Choose the word that finishes the sentence and write it on the lines.

_____

_____ we left on our trip, I said good-bye to my cat.

Before/Soon

_____

We got on the train and _____ it started down the tracks.

soon/here

_____

My mom said, "Come over _____ You can sit

there/here

by the window."

_____

I'm glad I did. _____ was a lot to see along the way.

There/Here

Riddle Time

Use the words from the box to finish each riddle.

Word Box

where   now   open

I'm a verb that tells what you do
with doors, and books, and eyes—it's true!

_____

- - - - - - - - - - - - - - - - -

Who am I? _____

A sign, address, directions, or map—

_____

- - - - - - - - - - - - - - -

they all tell you _____ things are at.

This minute! Right away! Anyhow,

_____

- - - - - - - - - - - - -

they really mean the same thing: "right _____!"

A-Maze-ing!

Follow the path of words with the question words.

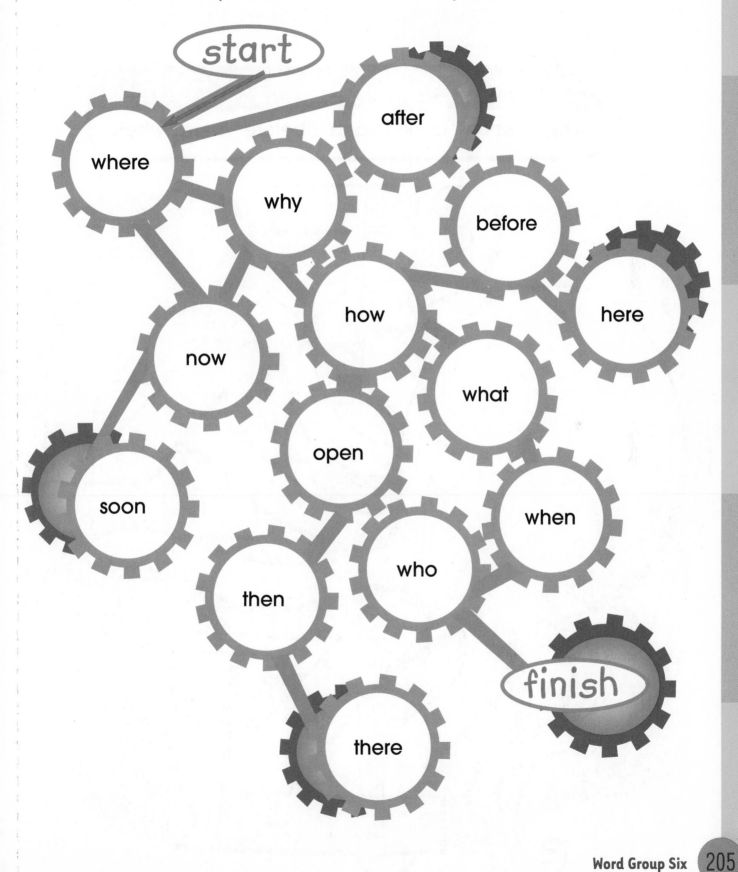

Every Which Way

Write the words that fit in the arrows. Choose from the words in the box. Some words appear more than once.

Word Box

why   when   open   soon   before   here   where

Magic W's

How many words can you make from the letters in these **w** words? Give yourself three minutes to write as many as you can!

why

where

what

when

-hat- -her-

Piece It Together

Draw lines to match the first syllables to the second syllables.

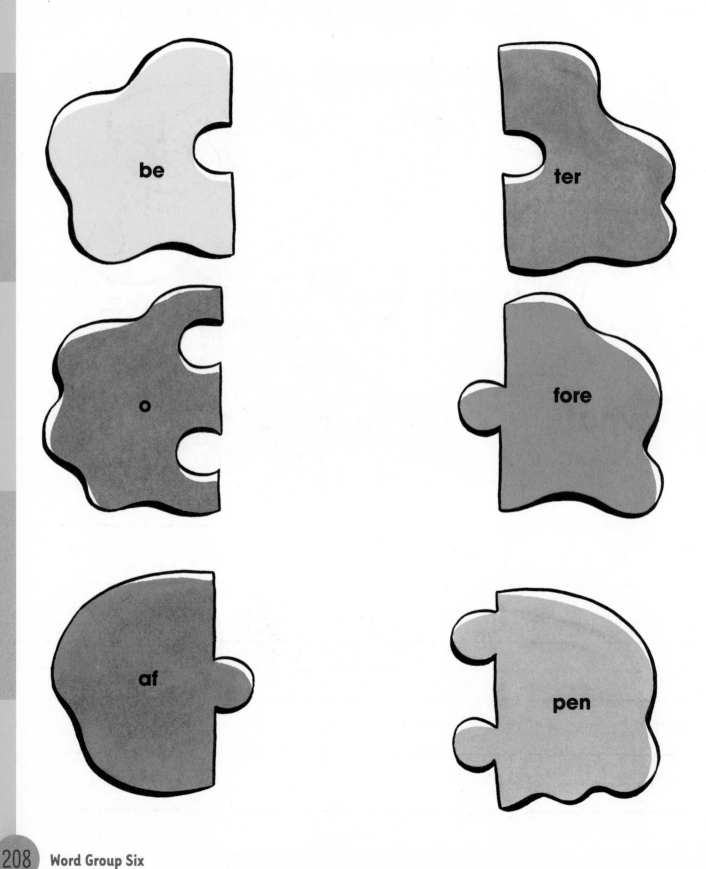

be

ter

o

fore

af

pen

Catch Up!

Help the cat catch up with the mouse.
Write the words that fit in each step.

Word Box

how	why	what	then
when	open	soon	now

Wake Up!

Pretend you took a nap that lasted 100 years! Use **after**, **before**, **open**, **now** to write three sentences about what happened when you woke up.

Alphabet River

Help Kisha cross the brook! Put these words in alphabetical order on the stones.

Word Box

what
open
soon
then
now
when
after
before
here
how

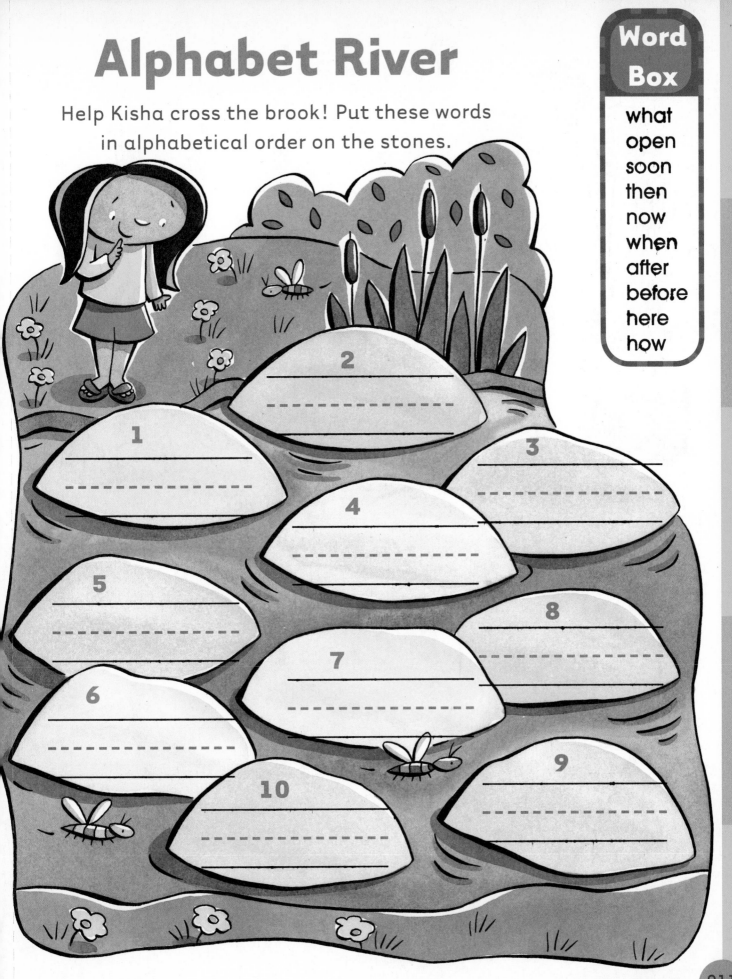

Opposites

Draw lines to connect the opposites.

here	before
after	closed
good-bye	hello
open	then
many	there
now	few

Here to There

The path of words that are spelled correctly
will get you from here to there.

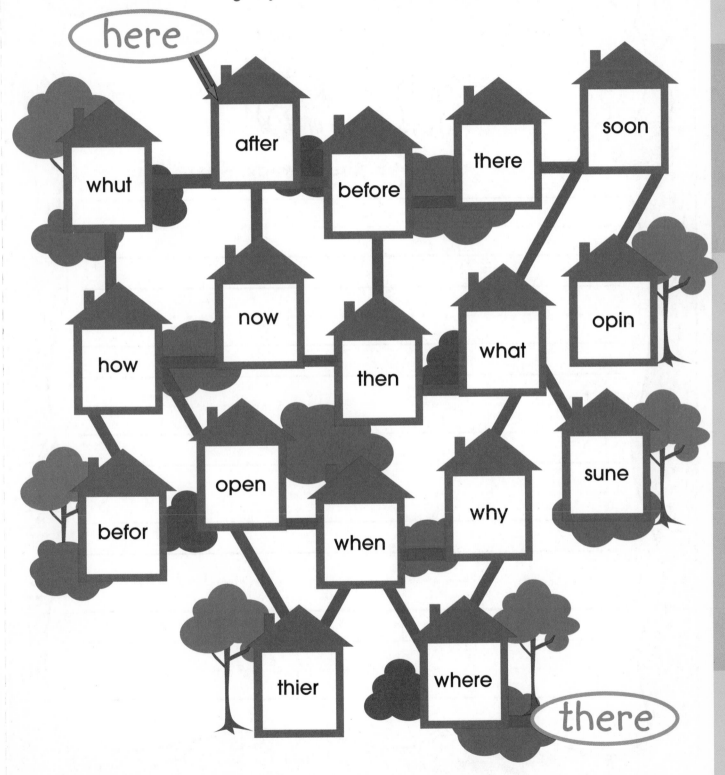

here

here · after · before · there · soon

whut · now · what · opin

how · then · sune

befor · open · why · when

thier · where

there

BOOO!

Write your own spooky story. You are the main character. Here are the other characters:

Use these words: **who**, **there**, **what**, **where**, **why**.

Questions, Questions

Read the poem. Then circle all the words
that begin with (wh).

Before and after,
Now, soon, then.
Five little words
that tell you when.

Here and there
will tell you where.

Got another question?
Try who or why
or how or what —
And don't be shy!

Word Group 6   Answer Key

185 1. how; 2. now; 3. open; 4. here; 5. Soon; 6. Before, after

186 1. where; 2. what; 3. When; 4. why; 5. then; 6. there; answers will vary

187 **Who:** several children; **What:** a pot of gold; **When:** yesterday; **Where:** in a faraway field; **Why:** to see if there was gold at the end; **How:** they followed the rainbow

188 What; Where; When; Why

189 1. after; 2. after; 3. after; 4. after; 5. before

190 **Down:** 1. where; 2. what; **Across:** 1. why; 2. When

191 Choose among so, on, no; he, her; we, here, her; be, bee, for, or; the, he, hen, net; here, her, he, the

192 how; what; then; soon

193 1. n; 2. e; 3. r; 4. a; fingernails

194 here; here; there; there; here; here; there

195 **Question words:** when; how; why; where; who; what; **Words that tell when:** now; soon; then; after; before

196 who; here; why; then

197 Why; When; What; How

198 1. opened; 2. open house; 3. out in the open; 4. opening; 5. open

199 see right; mermalade

200 now/soon; here/there; before/after

201 draw lines to match text to photos

202 circle dog; open; soon; why; how

203 Before; soon; here; There

204 open; where; now

205 see right

206 see right

207 answers will vary

208 be/fore; o/pen; af/ter

209 see right

210 answers will vary

211 1. after; 2. before; 3. here; 4. how; 5. now; 6. open; 7. soon; 8. then; 9. what; 10. when

212 here/there; after/before; good-bye/hello; open/closed; many/few; now/then

213 see right

214 answers will vary

215 circle: when; where; who; why; what

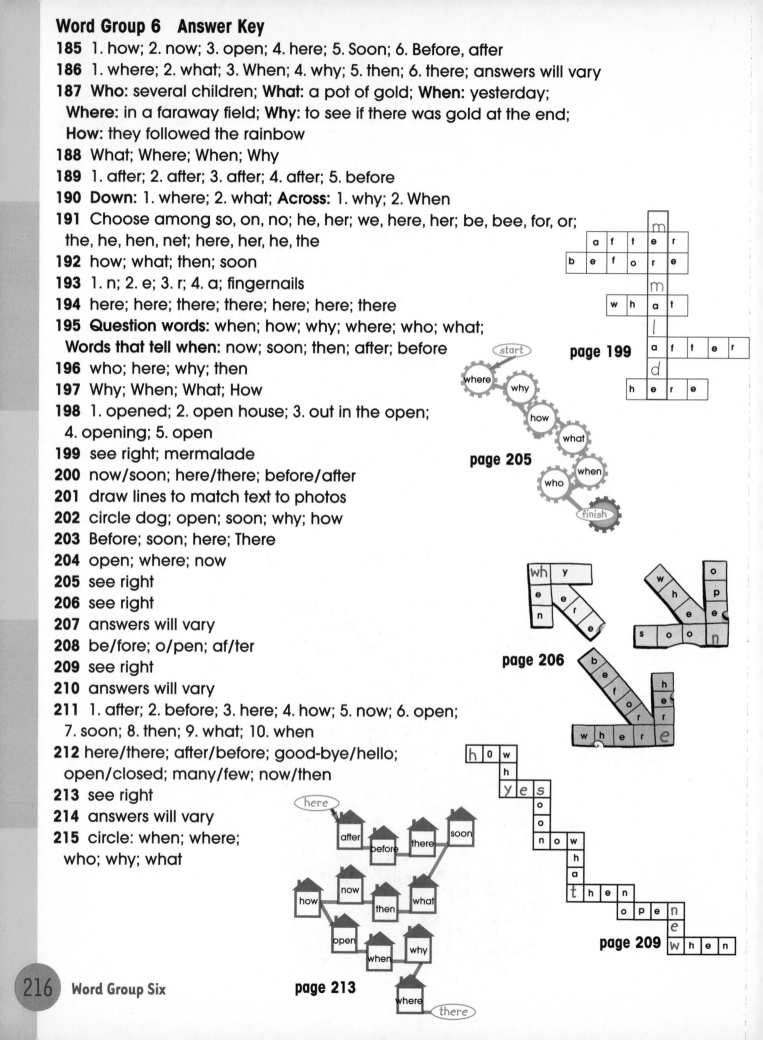

page 199

page 205

page 206

page 209

page 213

Just then, Sniffy and Ben saw Mrs. Bunny by the tree.

"How about some cake?" she said. "I made it with the big carrot I found."

"Ah-ha!" said Sniffy. "Now I know where to find that carrot. Let's eat!"

8

The Case of the Missing carrot

Written by Kathryn McKeon
Illustrated by Jackie Snider

1

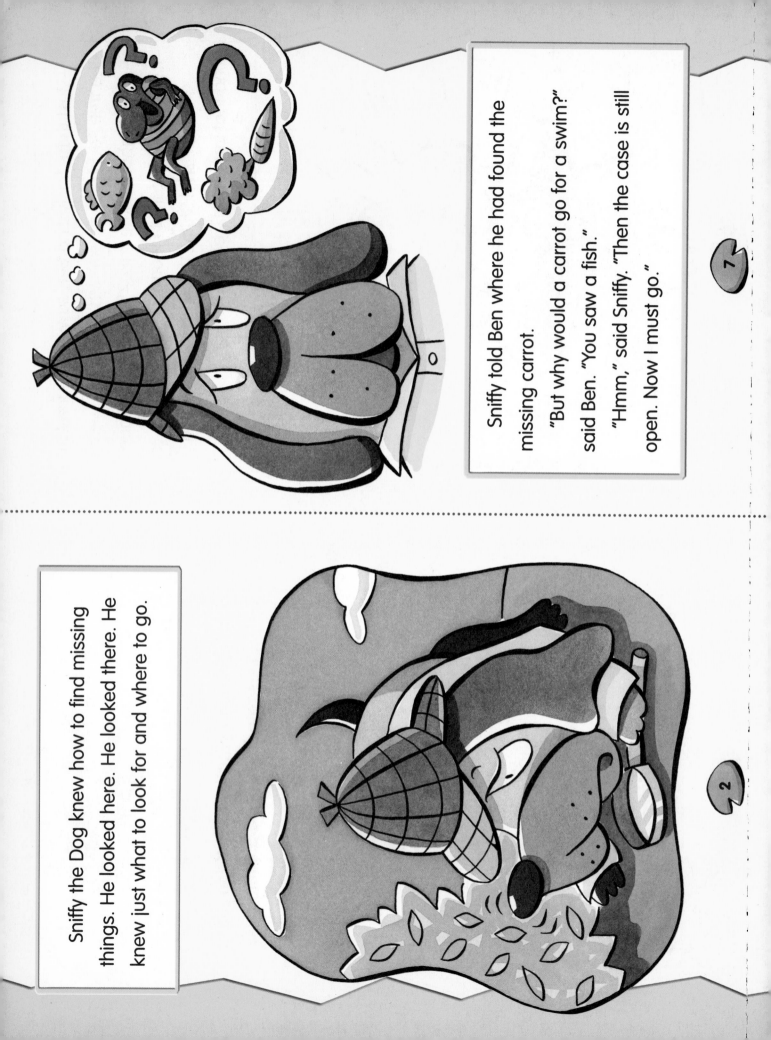

Sniffy told Ben where he had found the missing carrot.

"But why would a carrot go for a swim?" said Ben. "You saw a fish."

"Hmm," said Sniffy. "Then the case is still open. Now I must go."

Sniffy the Dog knew how to find missing things. He looked here. He looked there. He knew just what to look for and where to go.

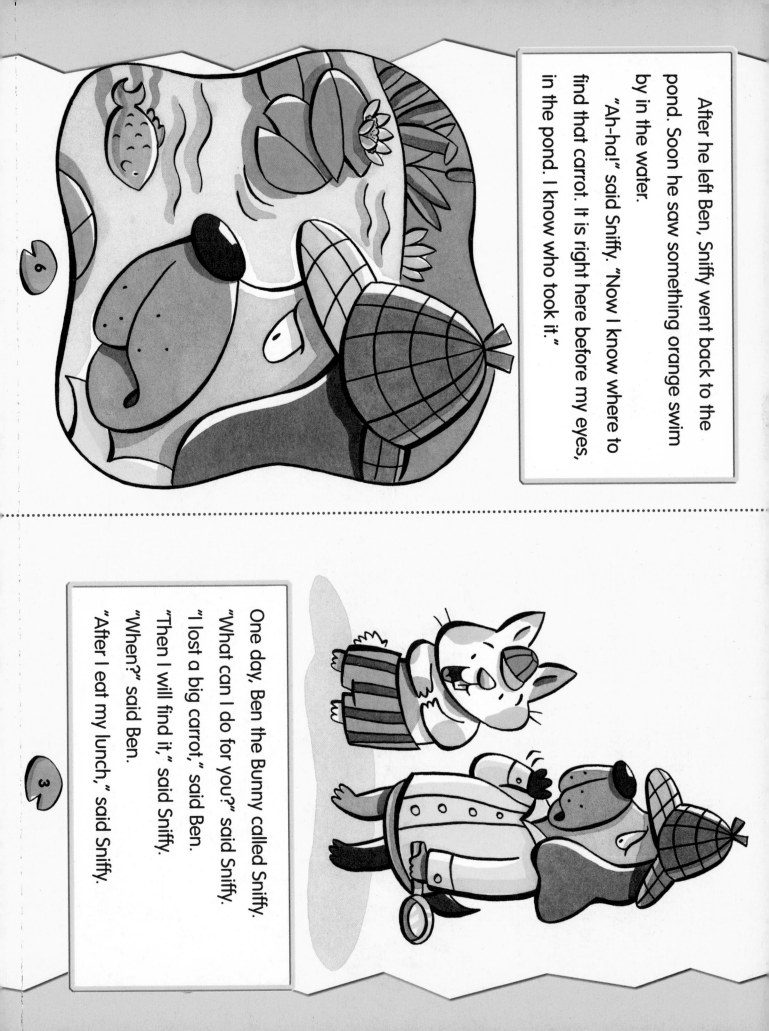

After he left Ben, Sniffy went back to the pond. Soon he saw something orange swim by in the water.

"Ah-ha!" said Sniffy. "Now I know where to find that carrot. It is right here before my eyes, in the pond. I know who took it."

9

One day, Ben the Bunny called Sniffy.
"What can I do for you?" said Sniffy.
"I lost a big carrot," said Ben.
"Then I will find it," said Sniffy.
"When?" said Ben.
"After I eat my lunch," said Sniffy.

3

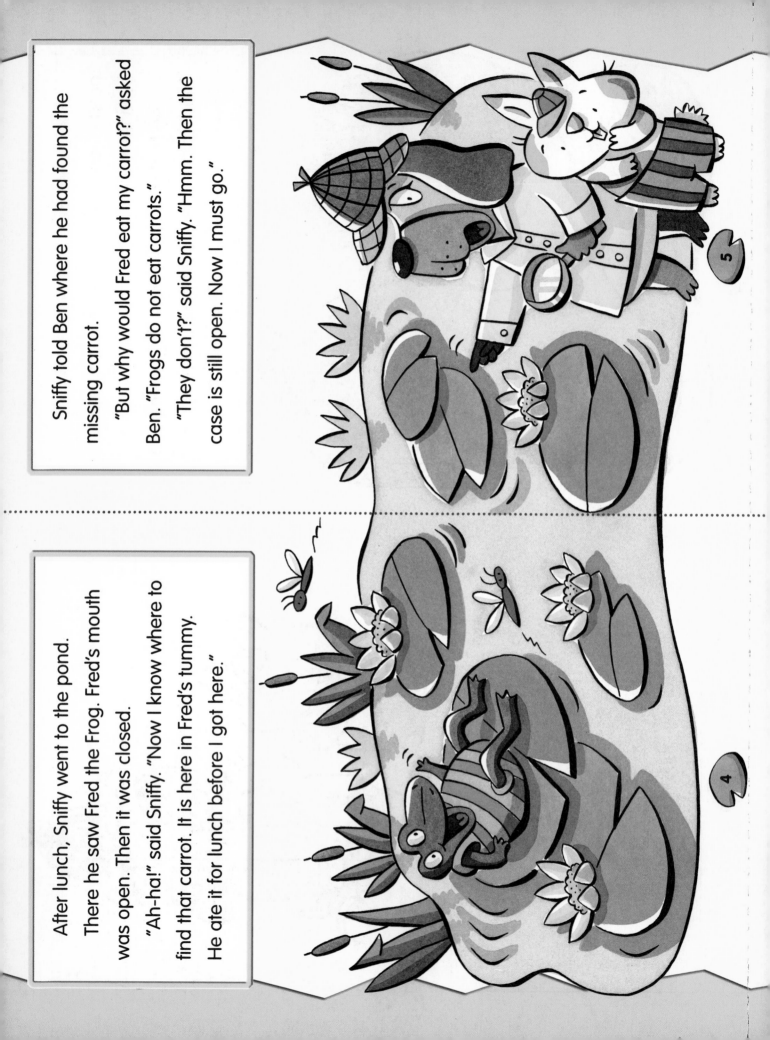

Sniffy told Ben where he had found the missing carrot.

"But why would Fred eat my carrot?" asked Ben. "Frogs do not eat carrots."

"They don't?" said Sniffy. "Hmm. Then the case is still open. Now I must go."

5

After lunch, Sniffy went to the pond. There he saw Fred the Frog. Fred's mouth was open. Then it was closed.

"Ah-ha!" said Sniffy. "Now I know where to find that carrot. It is here in Fred's tummy. He ate it for lunch before I got here."

4

Word Search

Fill in the blanks with the right words from the box.

Word Box

early   fall   into   over

end   fell   more

The opposite of late is _____ .

After summer comes _____ .

The dog crawled _____ his little house.

The boy tripped and _____ down.

The opposite of less is _____ .

The opposite of under is _____ .

The opposite of beginning is _____ .

What's the Story?

Finish the sentences with
the words from the word box.

Word Box

quiet   under
spring   wide
story   Winter
Summer

_____

The opposite of loud is _____ .

_____

After winter comes _____ .

_____

_____ is the coldest season.

_____

The opposite of over is _____ .

_____

The opposite of narrow is _____ .

_____

My favorite bedtime _____ is *Cinderella*.

_____

_____ is the warmest season.

Season Sentences

Word Box

winter   summer
spring   fall

After each phrase, write the season in which you'd be most likely to find that thing.

a new school year _____

long vacation _____

snowman _____

new flowers _____

suntan lotion _____

snowflakes _____

last day of school _____

red, orange, and yellow leaves _____

The Silly Snowman

Read the story. Then read the sentences below and circle **true** or **false**.

Once there was a silly snowman. He didn't like the cold.

He didn't like winter. He wanted to go to the beach in the summer.

The silly snowman padded himself with snow all winter.

He got very big and very round.

When spring came, he snuck into a store. He hid in the freezer.

He waited for summer.

When summer came, the silly snowman headed for the beach.

It was a very short trip!

The snowman liked winter.	true	false
The snowman got very big.	true	false
The snowman hid in a house.	true	false
The snowman hid in a freezer.	true	false
The snowman stayed at the beach for the whole summer.	true	false

Where Is It?

Circle (under) or (over) to finish the sentences.

The road is (under, over) the car.

The roof is (under, over) the house.

The girl is (under, over) the umbrella.

Her hand is (under, over) her head.

Now, write your own sentences:

The _____ is **over** the _____.

The _____ is **under** the _____.

Picture This!

Draw a line to match the sentences to the pictures.

She puts more ice cream into her bowl.

The cat is under the table.

Please be quiet!

He reads a story before he falls asleep.

Over or Under?

Look at the picture. Write **over** or **under** on the lines to tell if the things are over the bed or under the bed.

picture of puppies _____

shoes _____

boxes _____

a first-prize ribbon _____

sign that says **Maria's Room** _____

Silly Snakes

Joe's pet snakes are driving him crazy! Look at the picture. Fill in the blanks with the right words from the box.

Word Box

over   more   wide   into   under   fell

_____

There are three snakes _____ the bed.

_____

There are _____ snakes in the closet!

_____

One snake is hanging _____ the lampshade!

_____

One snake is so _____, he is blocking the door.

_____ _____

One snake _____ _____ the fishbowl!

Mouse Mischief

This little mouse took some letters and hid them in his mouse house! In each set of words, the same letter is missing. Write the missing letter at the end of each set.

1. __ ore _____

su __ __ er _ _ _ _

The missing letter is _____ .

2. __ nto

qu __ et

spr __ ng

w __ de _____

w __ nter _ _ _ _

The missing letter is _____ .

3. __ arly

__ nd

f __ ll

mor __

ov __ r

qui __ t

summ __ r

und __ r

wid __ _____

wint __ r _ _ _ _

The missing letter is _____ .

4. ea __ ly

mo __ e

sp __ ing

sto __ y

summe __

unde __ _____

winte __ _ _ _ _

The missing letter is _____ .

5. __ pring

__ tory _____

__ ummer _ _ _ _

The missing letter is _____ .

Now write all the missing letters on the lines.
They spell out the answer to the riddle!

What do cats like to eat for breakfast?

_____ _____ _____ _____

_ _ _ _ _ _ _ _ _ _ _ _ _ _ _ _ _ _ _ _

_____ _____ c _____ c _____ p _____

  1   2   3   4   2   5   2   3   5

The Early Bird

Read this saying. What do you think it means?

The early bird catches the worm.

Now use the words from the box
to make up new sayings about birds!

Word Box

pretty   quiet   small   wide

1. The _____ bird gets the most room in the nest.

2. The _____ bird is not singing.

3. The _____ bird wears a bow in its hair.

4. The _____ bird can easily hide.

Pack It Up!

Put all the season words from the word box in the trunk on the left. Put all the adjectives (describing words) in the trunk on the right.

Word Box

fall	spring	summer	winter
wide	quiet	early	

Season Words

_____

- - - - - - - - - - -

_____

- - - - - - - - - - -

_____

- - - - - - - - - - -

_____

- - - - - - - - - - -

Adjectives

_____

- - - - - - - - - - -

_____

- - - - - - - - - - -

_____

- - - - - - - - - - -

Flying High

Write the word that rhymes with all the words on that kite's tail. Choose from the words in the box.

tried

side

tied

slide

bride

blue

grew

who

two

too

door

sore

four

store

roar

shell

bell

sell

spell

well

Season Riddles

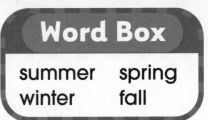
Word Box

summer   spring
winter   fall

Finish the riddles with words from the box.

Fun and sun—vacation, too.
I'm a time when skies are blue.
Which season am I?

_____

_ _ _ _ _ _ _ _ _ _ _ _ _ _ _ _

_____

Flowers and rain, umbrellas and sun
That's how you know I have begun.
Which season am I?

_____

_ _ _ _ _ _ _ _ _ _ _ _ _ _ _

_____

Skiing and snowmen,
warm clothes to wear.
Cocoa and holidays,
and trees are bare.
Which season am I?

_____

_ _ _ _ _ _ _ _ _ _ _ _ _ _ _

_____

New colors for leaves, a new school year,
And on the trees, red apples appear.
Which season am I?

_____

_ _ _ _ _ _ _ _ _ _ _ _ _ _

_____

Fives & Sixes

Use the words from the word box to answer these questions.

Word Box

early	spring	under	summer
quiet	story	winter	

1. Which 6-letter word starts with the same sound as spin?

_____

- - - - - - - - - - - - - -

_____

2. Which 5-letter word is the opposite of late? _____

_____

- - - - - - - - - - - - - -

3. Which 5-letter word is the opposite of loud? _____

_____

- - - - - - - - - - - - - -

4. Which 5-letter word is the opposite of over? _____

5. Which 5-letter word starts with the same sound as stairs?

_____

- - - - - - - - - - - - - -

_____

6. Which 6-letter word ends with starts with s and ends with r?

_____

- - - - - - - - - - - - - -

_____

7. Which 6-letter word ends in the same sound as sister?

_____

- - - - - - - - - - - - - -

_____

Stacking Up!

Write the words from the box in the spaces where they fit.
Hint: One word is used twice. Then answer the riddle
by writing the letters in the red boxes on the line.

Word Box

quiet   story   fall   more   summer

What did the duck want with his soup?

_____

- -

_____

What a Pair!

Fill the boxes with words that fit.
Choose from the words in the box.
Hint: Each puzzle contains two words
that are a pair.

Word Box

fell	under	winter
fall	over	summer

It's a Spring Thing

Finish the sentences with words
from the word box.

Tina loves to swing in the _____ . She gets up

_____ every day, when it is still _____ in

the neighborhood, and sits on her _____ wooden

swing. She wants to go high and go _____ the branch,

but she can't because she would _____ off! She swings

until the _____ of the day. Tina feels like she has wings!

Five Times, Fast!

Fill in the blanks in the tongue twisters so they
make sense. Choose from the words in the box.
Then say them each five times out loud . . . and fast!

Word Box

fell   winter   summer

Susan's favorite seasons are

_____

spring and _____.

Fran _____ into the fall leaves.

Wayne wants _____ clothes.

Summer Vacation

Finish the sentences with words
from the word box.

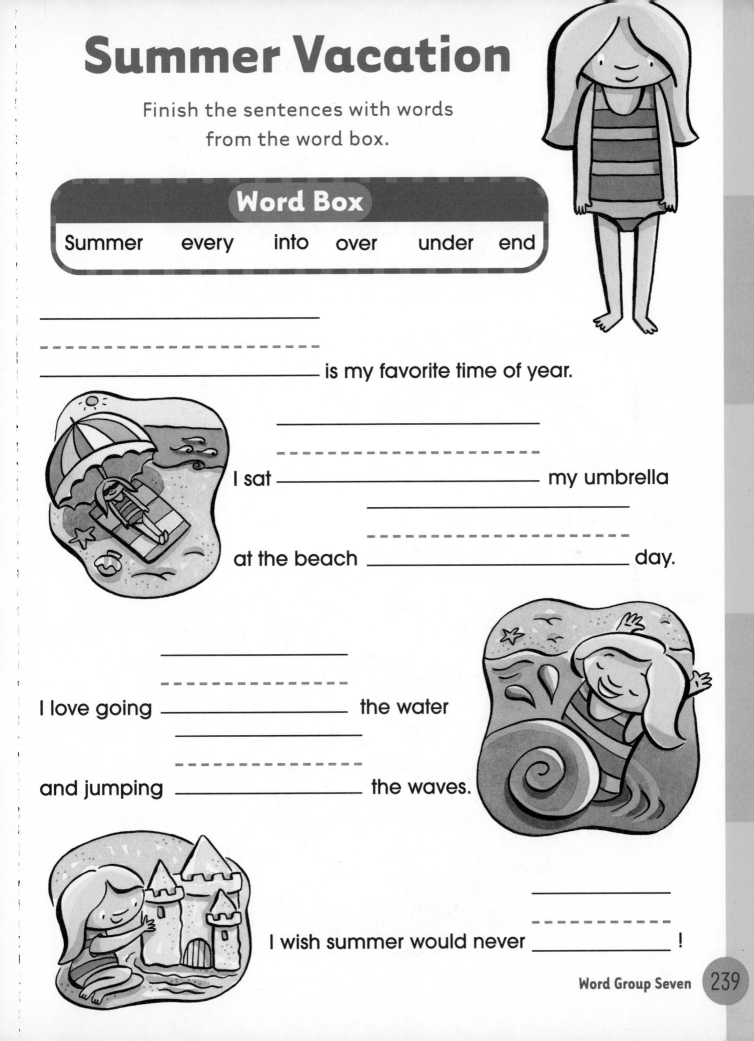

Word Box

Summer   every   into   over   under   end

_____

- -

_____ is my favorite time of year.

_____

- -

I sat _____ my umbrella

_____

- -

at the beach _____ day.

_____

- - - - - - - - - - - - - - - - - -

I love going _____ the water

_____

- - - - - - - - - - - - - - - - - -

and jumping _____ the waves.

_____

- - - - - - - - - - - - - - -

I wish summer would never _____ !

Spelling Patrol

Circle the word in each group that is spelled correctly.
Put an X on the words that are spelled incorrectly.

erly	early	earley
kwiet	quiet	queit
under	undir	ander
wid	wide	whyde
sumer	summer	summir

Juggling Syllables

The clown on the left is juggling the first syllables of each word.
The clown on the right is juggling the second syllables. Put the
correct syllables together and write the words on the lines.

A-Maze-ing Adjectives

Follow the path of adjectives (describing words).

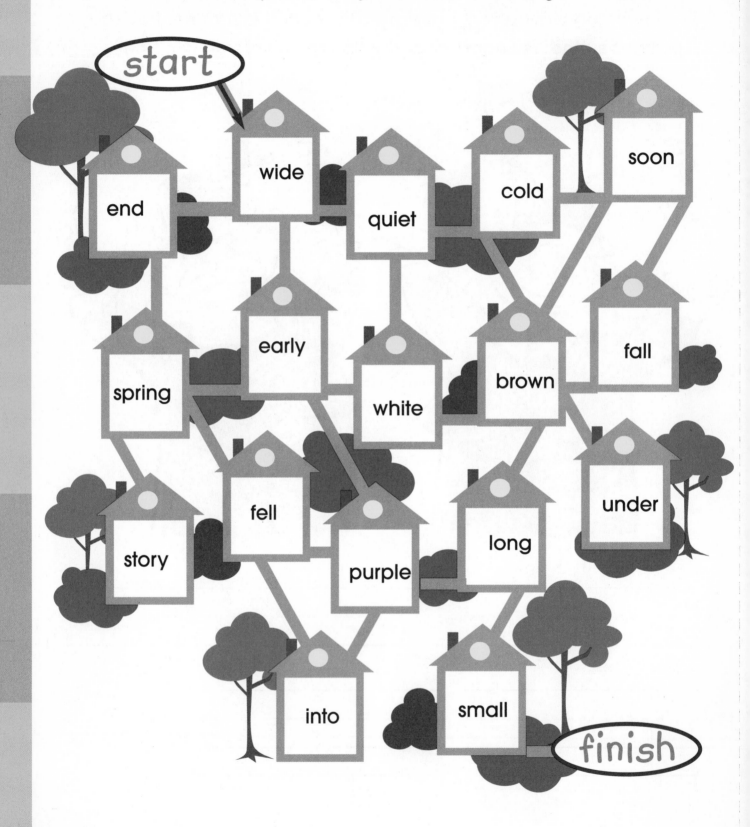

Every Which Way

Write the words that fit in the arrows. Choose from the words in the box. One season word is used twice.

Word Box

summer   under   winter   spring   story

Crossword Fun

Word Box

story   more   over   end   early   summer

Choose from the words in the box to complete the puzzle.

Across

1. Will you read me a

_____ ?

2. I woke up _____

today.

4. The opposite of under is

_____ .

5. The opposite of beginning is

_____ .

Down

1. The warmest season is

_____

3. The opposite of less is

_____

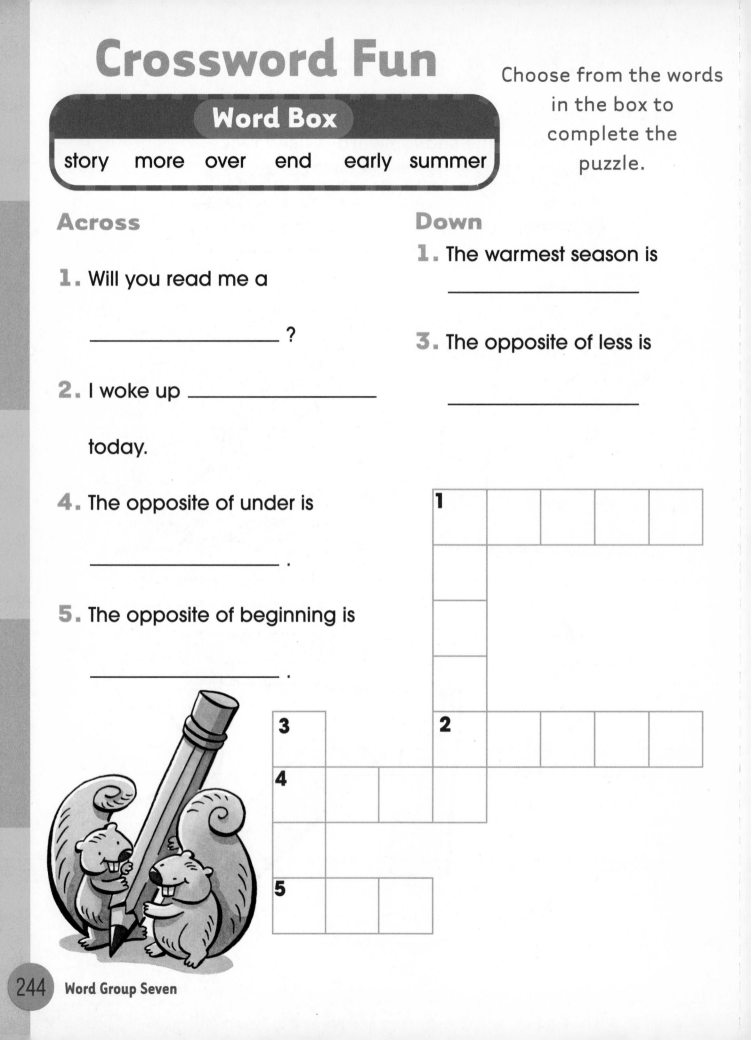

A Whole Year of Words

How many words can you make from the letters in these season words? Write as many as you can!

Winter Summer Spring Fall

ten	rip	

Looks Like Snow!

Use the words from the box to finish the weather report.

Word Box

Early	winter
fell	more
end	under
wide	quiet

_____

Snow _____ all day yesterday. It felt like it would

never _____ . _____ this morning,

the whole town looked like a _____ wonderland,

far and _____ . All was _____

outside. Houses, cars, and trees were buried _____

a blanket of snow! We predict _____ snow

tomorrow! Have fun!

Get Over It!

Read the sentences. Then choose
the word from the box that fits.
Write it in the blank.

Word Box

overflow   oversleep
overcoat   overlaps
overboard

1. In the fall I wear a warm _____ .

2. To fall off a ship is to fall _____ .

3. When you put one thing a little bit on top of another thing,

   _____

   it _____ .

4. Don't put too much water in the bathtub,

   _____

   it might _____ !

5. To sleep too late is to _____ .

A, B, C Bubbles

Help the scuba diver come up! Put these words
in alphabetical order on the bubbles.

Word Box

winter	under	over	into
~~early~~	fall	spring	summer
wide	quiet	more	fell
~~end~~		story	

1 early

2 end

3

4

5

6

7

8

9

10

11

12

13

14

Outer Space Spelling Bee Board Game

You'll Need:

- the game board on pages 250–251
- a number cube or die
- a game piece for each player (coins or beans will work)
- pencil and paper for each player

How to Play

1. Roll the number cube. Move your piece the number of dots in the cube.

2. If you land on a planet, read the sentence and then write the answer on your paper. Have another player check your answer. If you land on a star, read the word out loud, then turn around and write it on your paper. (Check your answer by turning around and matching what you wrote to the word on the star.) If you answer correctly, take another turn.

3. The first person to reach FINISH wins!

Outer Space Spelling Bee

Be an astronaut. Try to land on the moon!

Start

winter

Spell the word that is the opposite of narrow.

early

Spell the name of the coldest season.

wide

Spell the word that is the opposite of late.

end

fall

under

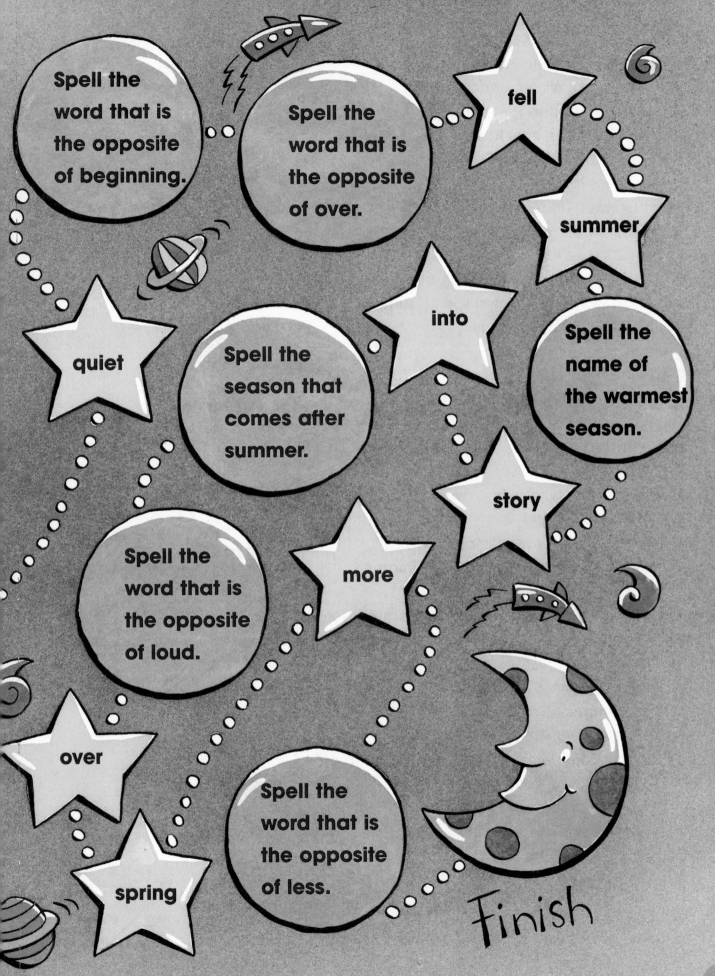

Word Group 7 Answer Key

221 early; fall; into; fell; more; over; end

222 quiet; spring; Winter; under; wide; story; Summer

223 fall; summer; spring; winter; winter; summer; summer; fall

224 false; true; false; true; false

225 under; over; under; over; answers will vary

226 draw lines to connect text to photos

227 over; under; under; over; over

228 under; more; over; wide; fell; into

229 1. m; 2. i; 3. e; 4. r; 5. s; mice crispies

230 1. wide; 2. quiet; 3. pretty; 4. small,

231 **Season Words:** fall; winter; spring; summer

   Adjectives: wide; quiet; early

232 wide; into; fell; more

233 summer; spring; winter; fall

234 1. spring; 2. early; 3. quiet; 4. under; 5. story;

   6. summer; 7. winter

235 see right; quackers

236 see right

237 spring; early; quiet; wide; over; fall; end

238 summer; fell; winter

239 Summer; under; every; into; over; end

240 circle early; quiet; under; wide; summer;

   X all other words

241 summer; quiet; under; winter; into; early; over

242 see right

243 see right

244 **Across:** 1. story; 2. early; 4. over; 5. end

   Down: 1. summer; 3. more

245 answers will vary

246 fell; end; Early; winter; wide; quiet; under; more

247 1. overcoat; 2. overboard; 3. overlaps;

   4. overflow; 5. oversleep

248 1. early; 2. end; 3. fall; 4. fell; 5. into; 6. more; 7. over;

   8. quiet; 9. spring; 10. story; 11. summer;

   12. under; 13. wide; 14. winter

page 235

page 236

start

wide
quiet
cold
early
white
brown
purple
long
small
finish

page 242

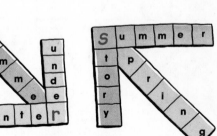

page 243

The story of the seasons goes 'round.
Changing things here on the ground.
And every season, I wish on a star.
And hope my wish goes up that far.

8

fold & assemble

The Seasons

written by
Gail Tuchman

Scholastic 100 Words Kids Need to
Read by 2nd Grade, Word Group 7

1

Summer sea, so wide and blue,
It looks like there is no end to you.
I fell into your cool, cool water.
And when more waves came,
I dived under.

Yellow, orange, purple, red.
Fall leaves piled into a great big bed.
Wide leaves, thin ones, large and small.
Jump into color. Jump into fall!

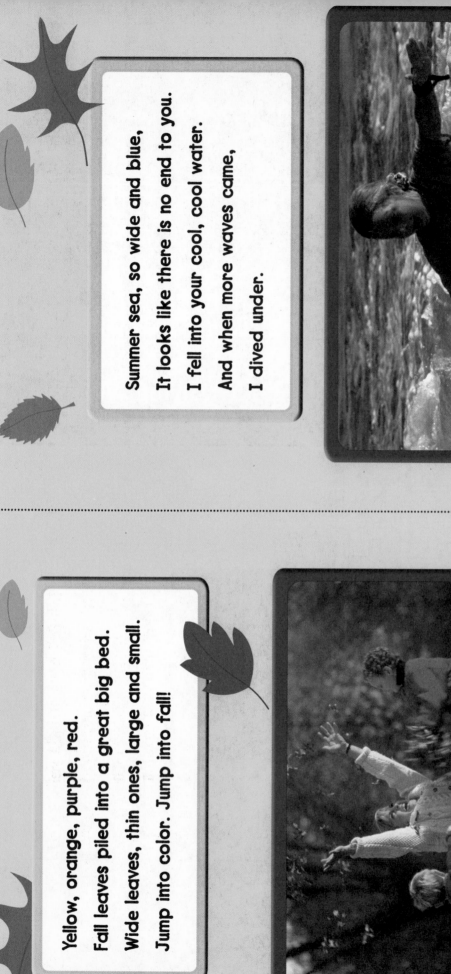

Spring rains fall over the earth below.
Now spring flowers, grow, grow, grow.
Sun kisses the earth. Winter's gone away.
Spring turns into hot summer days.

6

Tall fall corn stands yellow and high.
Fat, orange pumpkins turn into pie.
Fall's purple grapes and fall's green peas,
dance with red apples falling from trees.

3

Bears wake up. Bees buzz in.

Butterflies open their wide, bright wings.

Early birds start singing,

"Hello, spring."

Fall turns to winter, winter white.

Days end early, then it is night.

Snow keeps falling over everything.

All is quiet.

The earth waits for spring.